SELF-
HYP

"Whether you believe you can do a thing or not, you are right."

Henry Ford (1863 – 1947)

Printed in Victoria, BC, Canada

Note for Librarians: a cataloguing record for this book that includes Dewey Decimal Classification and US Library of Congress numbers is available from the Library and Archives of Canada. The complete cataloguing record can be obtained from their online database at:
www.collectionscanada.ca/amicus/index-e.html
ISBN 1-4120-4532-0

TRAFFORD

This book was published *on-demand* in cooperation with Trafford Publishing. On-demand publishing is a unique process and service of making a book available for retail sale to the public taking advantage of on-demand manufacturing and Internet marketing. On-demand publishing includes promotions, retail sales, manufacturing, order fulfilment, accounting and collecting royalties on behalf of the author.

Offices in Canada, USA, UK, Ireland, and Spain
***book sales for North America and international*:**
Trafford Publishing, 6E–2333 Government St.
Victoria, BC V8T 4P4 CANADA
phone 250 383 6864   toll-free 1 888 232 4444
fax 250 383 6804   email to orders@trafford.com

***book sales in Europe*:**
Trafford Publishing (UK) Ltd., Enterprise House, Wistaston Road Business Centre
Crewe, Cheshire CW2 7RP UNITED KINGDOM
phone 01270 251 396   local rate 0845 230 9601
facsimile 01270 254 983   orders.uk@trafford.com

***order online at*:**
www.trafford.com/robots/04-4120.html

10   9   8   7   6   5   4   3   2   1

SELF-CHANGE
HYPNOSIS

"Well, I liken this to an oil painting: Imagine that when you are born you are a blank canvas, with just faint pencil lines marking out your genetics and DNA. Every minute from now on your painting starts to take shape. Everything you see, hear and experience is recorded on your canvas. And slowly and surely you grew into the masterpiece you are today!"

RICHARD MACKENZIE

FOR JACKEÉ

"You are my sunshine, my rock and the secret of my success"

Acknowledgements

I would like to thank all the people who helped me to create this book...

Olf Stoiber for being a good friend and colleague and for doing such a great foreword.

My biggest thank-you has to go to my clients. Each and every person I work with means more to me than they could ever know.

Contents

Foreword

"Reading this book might be one of the most valuable time investments you have ever made! And the reason for that is very simple: Instead of just telling you what to do in order to achieve your personal goals, Richard MacKenzie is about to show you how to find out for yourself. And he gives you all you need in order to do so over and over again, on a long-term, consistent basis."

Olf Stoiber

Foreword

I believe there is a reason why you have picked up this book. Maybe you want to find out more about your own mind, learning how to use it efficiently. Maybe you have a specific area in your life where problems have troubled you and you feel it's about time to change that now. But most likely you are at a point in your life where you have decided to take charge of your own mind and make it work for you – instead of just dealing with what life throws at you. Let me congratulate you: Reading this book might be one of the most valuable time investments you have ever made! And the reason for that is very simple: Instead of just telling you what to do in order to achieve your personal goals, Richard MacKenzie is about to show you how to find out for yourself. And he gives you all you need in order to do so over and over again, on a long-term, consistent basis.

There is one common situation most hypnotherapists have to deal with in their day-to-day work: clients who want to be "fixed", who want the therapist to solve all their problems. Even though this might work in some cases, there are some serious downsides to that sort of practice. First of all, the client becomes dependent. The therapist might be able to solve one problem for you, but the next problem is waiting just around the corner – and what then? You might become one of the therapy-junkies we encounter so often these days. Instead of learning the skills of how to handle your own life, you want someone else to do it for you. Chances are you'll never become liberated, free and happy.

A good therapist will approach things differently. He will refuse to be your problem-fixer. Instead, he'll give you the tools and show you the way to make your life better yourself. It's all about self-empowerment, and I believe this could be considered one of the most respectful and powerful therapies available. You'll benefit from it for your entire life – no matter what your problem was in the first place. You will mature to a person who is more and more able to handle things on his or her own, and become happier, healthier and probably wealthier in the process. Now that's what I call real therapy!

To take things one step further: The expression "therapy" is sometimes overused. Sometimes it's just small changes you need in order to feel better and more fulfilled. And at other times, you might just need some inspiration or a helping hand. If you feel self-empowered, you'll be able to deal confidently with almost everything you're faced with in life. Learn how to use your own brain and you will learn how to take charge of your own life – no matter if it's small problems or the chunkier ones you'll sometimes face.

As time keeps ticking on and we're advancing further into this millennium, more and more people discover the joy and benefits of doing something that should be taught at school. And the crème de la crème of self-empowerment is hypnosis! I've seen clients who have been deeply troubled in their lives and who didn't know how to possibly carry on. After having discovered the gift of hypnosis and having been taught how to facilitate this exciting state of mind, some of them experienced instant change. Some of them felt like getting better day by day until they've been able to live the way they have always dreamed of. What about you? Are there any goals you are striving to achieve? Is there anything in your life that could use a bit of improvement? The best thing about improving yourself is that your environment also benefits from it: Self-change is contagious; people around you will probably notice a more positive attitude about you – or just experience an additional portion of joy in life. By becoming a more fulfilled person yourself, you also help all the people around you to become happier – isn't this wonderful?

Richard MacKenzie is one of the leading British experts in working self-change miracles. The clients he sees in his Oxford hypnotherapy practice profit immensely from his guidance and skills. Now Richard has decided to make his vast knowledge and expertise available to anyone. In an easy-to-understand, fun-to-read style he equips you with the tools necessary to do powerful self-change work. It doesn't really matter whether you want to improve your health, stop smoking, earn more money or just want to be happier in general: Nobody will be able to achieve these results but you. For many people, the main question is: How? Why haven't things worked out for me in the past? If you happen to have asked these questions yourself, it's time to make a decision: Instead of asking yourself these numbing questions, ask yourself questions that empower you. Ask yourself: How can I make things work? And how can I have fun while doing so?

Starting from today, you could see life as an adventure. You never know where an adventure will lead you. You're faced with new situations every day. But instead of seeing them as problems, accept them and see them as opportunities to grow, to learn and to expand. And as it is with adventures: They are always fun! As is this book: You will enjoy reading it, and you will be able to make some lasting, powerful changes to the way you think, you feel and behave – could it get any better?

As a hypnotherapist and trainer myself, I have read my share of the many self-help books available. Some of them are not bad at all, and yet I was thrilled and motivated at the same time after having read Richard's book: Finally a book that doesn't stop by telling you what to do, but actually inspires you to do it!

Self-Change Hypnosis is probably one of the most valuable books you will ever read in your entire life. Read it and learn the skills. Practice, get better. Enjoy the process. And believe me, there are no limits to what you will achieve. Let Richard take you on the adventure of your life and allow him to be your guide – the changes you will experience will probably not be very far from miraculous!

Olf Stoiber
Munich, November 2004

Olf Stoiber is a hypnotherapist, coach and trainer who practices in Germany and in the UK. For more information, check out his Website at www.hypnoseberatung.de.

Introduction

"To accomplish great things, we must not only act, but also dream; not only plan, but also believe."

Anatole France (1844 – 1924)

Introduction

As a hypnotist and Personal Development Therapist, I see hundreds to thousands of clients each and every year in my private practice in Oxfordshire, in the United Kingdom. These clients come to me wishing to change certain aspects of their lives. They may wish to deal with straightforward things or maybe the major stuff, such as their relationships, their career or maybe a bad habit they may have acquired. I really thrive on seeing these clients, and every morning I love getting out of bed, having my coffee and breakfast and then making my way in to the office to see them; however, the bit I love most about my chosen career and vocation in life is that I am able to continually develop myself and create the life I dream of.

It is my belief that we now live in such amazing and exciting times. We are able to put men into space, travel to the continent in twenty minutes under the sea and many other exciting things. However, the best of all is that we now know so much of how the mind works and what makes us tick that we can ultimately decide the major outcomes in our lives and not just leave them to chance.

"Until you make the unconscious conscious, it will direct your life and you will call it fate."

Carl Jung (1875 – 1961)

This is quite a bold statement, but I totally 100% believe it. On the day that I finished my training in hypnotherapy and NLP, my partner Jackeé brought me a card, a bottle of bubbly and a little ornament. On the ornament, which still sits on my office desk, are the following statements which I read every morning:

"Believe in Yourself:
You are your greatest asset, there's nothing that you can't do.

No one can keep you from dreaming; only you can make them come true.

What you achieve is determined by the desire you possess.

There is no better feeling than the feeling of success.

Believe in who you are and what you do.
Don't leave things up to fate, it's strictly down to you."

Author Unknown

Personal development is all about you! Ask yourself a question: "Where would you like to be five years from now?" Just imagine if you could choose to be anything that you wanted to be! As the old saying goes, "If you keep doing the same today as you did yesterday, you will have the same tomorrow as you have today!" So is today the day you choose to do something different?

So many people each year have good intentions when buying self-help books, tapes and even going to seminars, but unfortunately most books only get half read, tapes get listened to once and then forgotten about and the hype of the seminars usually only lasts for a few days; we then tend to slip back into our old self and pick up where we left off. Sound familiar? This book aims to change all that by starting and finishing with you! An experience of self-hypnosis is different for everyone, and the best advice I could give you, is to just "go with the flow" and expect nothing, but experience everything. Hypnosis for you should be very special and very relaxing; expect nothing else to start with.

So can this book help you?

If you've ever wanted to be yourself, but just better at it, this book can lend a hand. If you've ever wanted to have more self-confidence, this book can help you out. If you've ever wanted to get better grades, learn better, accomplish more with your work and schedule your time better, this book can facilitate that change! Self-hypnosis is about imagining what you can improve in your life and focusing on reaching it. So the response is, yes this book can help you!

I have written this book with tremendous anticipation that the techniques I practice on a daily basis and use during therapy sessions with clients, will help you to achieve amazing results and to acquire the life you have always dreamt of. Read this book from cover to cover, then read it again and build into your everyday life the techniques which you will learn. The thing that I really want you to take away from this book is that hypnosis is a completely natural occurrence in our everyday life and by gaining knowledge in it, by anchoring and manipulating it, we can change our lives both internally and externally and get extraordinary results in a short amount of time. In your hands you hold the information that you require to become whatever you want. You may aspire to be a dustman, a teacher, a businessman or even the Chief Executive Officer of an international company – it's up to you! So take this book, put it to good use developing your life, and become the person that you have always wanted to become.

Richard MacKenzie
Self-Change Specialist & Author
Winter 2004

What Is Self-Hypnosis?

"Human beings, by changing the inner attitudes of their minds, can change the outer aspects of their lives."

William James (1842 - 1910)

What Is Self-Hypnosis?

Explaining to you what self-hypnosis is all about, is fortunately going to be really easy for me to do, as you have probably experienced self-hypnosis on some sort of level at least once already today! When, you are probably asking? Well have you driven today, had a chat with a boring person or been daydreaming? These are all common times when we tend to use hypnosis, which is also described as an altered state of consciousness.

If you drive, this will be very easy for you to understand. Try to remember the first time that you ever sat in the driver's seat, back in your first driving lesson. Try to remember all the things that you had to learn and then put into practice: putting your seat belt on, checking the mirrors, how to work the gears, remembering what all the peddles do and when to use them. It really was hard work and you had to rely on good concentration to enable you to learn and get the most out of the experience. Now take the last journey that you drove. Sure, you went from A to B just as when you were learning, but something was totally different this time. You conducted most if not your entire journey subconsciously, actually driving with the part of your mind that you don't consciously use. Now this sounds massively dangerous at first, but then you have to see that we tend to do a lot of things in life subconsciously. Take breathing, for instance: If you didn't do this subconsciously, don't you think that you might forget one day to take a breath? Now that's dangerous!

We have over time heard hypnosis and self-hypnosis described as many different weird and wonderful things. The truth is that hypnosis means different things to different people. There are, however, a few basics that seem to be the same throughout most beliefs about hypnosis: It is a relaxed state where the subconscious mind becomes easily accessible with a narrowing of the conscious mind. Hmmm! A bit technical, but don't get worried about that now as it will all fall into place later and become more obvious to you with time.

Now, when and in what areas of your life do you use hypnosis and self-hypnosis already? Well, let's look at daydreams to find out the answer to this question. We all tend to drift off at some point during the day and dream about things such as, what if I had a new job; or, I wonder if I can afford a nice holiday break in Hawaii, and sure enough for a few moments we're off living our dream in our heads as though we were on a different planet. So what is the point of daydreaming? Well, everything that you achieve starts with a thought, then it progresses into an idea and then into a dream and sure enough your mind starts to wonder off and the next thing you know is that you are off on another planet! These same ideas then sometimes start to become real events in your life. So you might ask, what has this got to do with self-hypnosis? As hypnotherapists we refer to daydreaming as "Forward Pacing".

Basically we know for a fact that almost everything that involves mankind achieving something starts with a single thought. This thought becomes an idea and then it follows through to become a dream, and then on to an ambition. Then with a little planning, "Wam-Bam-Thank-You-Mam" and you're living your dreams! Still not convinced? Then look at some really successful people, either someone you know or maybe someone you have read about in a newspaper or magazine. Now how do you think that they became successful? Maybe they had a huge bank balance handed to them by Mummy and Daddy or maybe, just maybe, they had a simple thought one day about designing a hoover that doesn't need a bag or building one of the world's biggest budget airlines, and made big bucks in the process. Surely you can think of someone like this, can't you? These people's current situations are directly linked to the thoughts, ideas and dreams that they chose to have sometime ago.

With all this in mind, remember the old saying "Be careful what you wish for as you might just get it!" We see this principle of "Forward Pacing" and daydreaming also breeding negative outcomes for people. After all, if it can be used for the good then be damn sure that it can be used for bad as well! A negative person doesn't wish or want bad things to happen, they just seem to! We all need to take great care in our ability to dream and make sure that we all give ourselves a happy ending.

Now in hypnotherapy I use "Forward Pacing" or "daydreaming" all the time while seeing my clients, and I will cover all you need to know about it in the following chapters, so that you too can achieve all that you could ever wish for!

Frequently Asked Questions Regarding Hypnosis

"A prudent question is one half of wisdom."

Francis Bacon (1561 - 1626)

Frequently Asked Questions Regarding Hypnosis

In this chapter I have answered some of the questions that I get asked most about hypnosis and hypnotherapy, by the general public. I aim to answer all the questions that you may have; however, if this is not the case, feel free to do some research on the Internet or check the MacKenzie Therapy & Training UK Website online at www.richardmackenzie.co.uk.

Can anyone use hypnosis?

The short answer to this question is, yes of course, anyone can use hypnosis. However, some people find it easier than others to achieve a deep level of hypnosis. Later in the book you will learn how to put yourself into a hypnotic trance. If you do have difficulty, just stay with it. It's true what they say, "Practice makes perfect". Even though hypnosis is a completely normal state, I am showing you these techniques to teach you how to anchor its power, how to use it when you want, not just when you use it naturally.

Important Note!
If you suffer from epilepsy or mental issues please consult your doctor before proceeding with hypnosis!

Is hypnosis dangerous?

As I have mentioned before, hypnosis is a completely natural state. We go into trance regularly on a day-to-day basis. I don't consider it to be dangerous whatsoever. You have probably heard stories about people being controlled while under hypnosis, well I'm afraid that is Hollywood's interpretation, and with no science to back it up. Certainly hypnosis is extremely successful, but only in getting you what you want. You can't be made in hypnosis to do anything that you don't want to, and you will feel completely comfortable the whole time. However, there are practical measures that you need to keep in mind. Obviously if you practice hypnosis in the car while driving with your eyes shut, then you might have a problem. Actually, it is not a good idea at all to listen to your recordings while driving.

What if I don't wake up?

Hypnosis is a completely ordinary and regular state and it cannot hold you against your will. If you were to go so deep as to enter a truly deep trance state, you would basically go into natural sleep and wake up when you were ready to do so. It is not possible for anyone to be "left" or "stuck" in hypnosis. During your practice time, if there were an emergency or something that needed your attention, you could easily awaken yourself at any time and simply stop.

What will it feel like?

It is an exclusive experience! Trance is a natural state that is comparable to that feeling you get just prior to falling asleep at night. When you wake up, you feel invigorated and rejuvenated as though you have had a long sleep. You just feel as if you are relaxing in a very contented space with your eyes closed. You can pay attention to everything, the sounds outside the building, a car going down the street outside, whatever. You have full awareness the whole time, conscious of everything going on around you as well as what your subconscious is revealing to you. I compare it to watching television in one room while a radio is on in another; you can transfer your awareness back and forth, switching between the two, absorbed in one but still conscious of the other.

How does hypnosis differ from meditation?

In meditation you do enter a trance; however, you just go with the flow and have little or no control over your experience. Hypnosis manipulates this trance state. You get to choose how deep you want to go and what you want to achieve while you are there. With hypnosis you guide yourself all the way through and remain in complete control.

How will I know that I have been in trance?

You will have to trust me on this one as everyone's experience of trance is different. If you are ever able to watch somebody go into trance then you will notice that their whole face seems to change. They look so relaxed and almost like they are a different person. Unfortunately you can not see this on yourself when you are in trance. You probably also will not be bothered to notice what your body feels like as your conscious mind will be somewhere else, almost feeling dissociated from your body. You will notice that it will be possibly the most relaxed that you have ever been before. You will also know because of the results that you get. If you are using hypnosis for a specific issue, you should notice improvements: The improvements themselves will let you know you have been in trance. Do not expect all bells and whistles because, as I keep saying, this is natural and you have experienced it thousands of times before. So just read, learn, relax and enjoy!

Can I hypnotise other people?

This book is not intended to teach you to become a therapist or a qualified hypnotist! Anyway to "hypnotise" someone you would have to have some sort of control over this person. It is a myth about hypnosis that the hypnotist has control over the client or subject. This is 100% false; all hypnosis is self-hypnosis, and that is to say you remain in complete control. If you are interested in training as a qualified hypnotherapist, be careful as there are a lot of courses out there that are not worth the investment of time and money. An excellent idea is to find a good hypnotherapist or hypnotherapy organisation and ask them where to train. You could also checkout the MacKenzie Therapy & Training UK Website at www.richardmackenzie.co.uk for more information.

When should I practice?

Personally I like to practice in the morning as this fits best into my day; also, as it is such a powerful tool, it is great to help you plan your day! However, you can practice when you wish, but it is a good idea to set a time and stick to it. Once you have been practising regularly you will soon notice how quickly it fits into your daily routine – and the more you practice, the more you will enjoy amazing results.

How long should I practice for?

Quality of time is more imperative than duration of time. Set aside some nominated time when you won't be bothered by anyone or anything, 15 to 20 minutes a day as a guide. Keep in mind that time spent committed to self-hypnosis is time invested in yourself to make constructive self-change, so practice frequently. Also, as you become more experienced you may find that you need a lesser amount of time.

How long does it take to get results with hypnosis?

The answer to this question is that it depends. Using hypnosis certainly speeds up the process of change and also makes that change much more successful. However, it does depend on how much work and time you put in. The other key factor is the issue that you are dealing with. With a little time you will be able to work through most issues, however with some you may need to seek professional help from a fully qualified hypnotherapist.

Induction Methods

"Live as if you were to die tomorrow. Learn as if you were to live forever."

Mahatma Gandhi (1869 – 1948)

Induction Methods

The aim of this chapter is to allow you to learn how to record your own voice to use as a guide in your own trance work. The advantage of having a recording is to ensure that a focus is kept and you don't drift off into a random day dream!

I use three steps in my self-hypnosis routine. First the "Induction": The aim here is to relax the body and begin to focus the mind on the task in hand. Second the "Deepener": This helps to relax the body even more and completely focuses the mind. It aims to use your imagination to occupy your conscious mind. This will help you into a deep level of trance. Third is "Coming Up": This is where you come out of trance and back to full awareness. All three areas will need to be on your recording.

How to make your recording

You will need a suitable tape recorder and a supply of recordable cassette tapes; alternatively, you may have the right software and equipment to make these recordings on your PC. Next find somewhere quiet where you will not be disturbed. The important message here is that the words you use really do not form much of the meaning compared to tone of voice. The way you sound can be much more relaxing than the words you use. Take time to play with your own voice. Notice that when you speed your voice up it takes more energy and is not at all relaxing; this is also the case for people listening to you. So on your recording, slow your voice right down and maybe make the tone a bit deeper. Where you see "..." in the script, it indicates that a pause for a few seconds is required. This will help you to feel more relaxed.

Progressive relaxation

Reading from a script can often sound unnatural compared to talking freely with basic guidelines. For this reason I am going to start with laying these basic guidelines for you, so that the whole process seems natural for you. There is also a scripted induction for you to use for the first couple of weeks until you feel that you can use these guidelines to create and tailor your own.

Guidelines

Draw all of your awareness to each part of your body in turn and visualise that area becoming so relaxed and comfortable. This can be helped by visualising in your mind a colour or liquid with "relaxing" properties flowing through your body. Envisage that your body is translucent and you can see within it. See it filling up with this tranquil fluid or colour. This can be thought of as cleansing in an emotional or spiritual sense; as so:

"Draw your attention to your feet...imagine what it would feel like if comfortable relaxing oil were flowing through them... See inside your body, as if it's transparent... See the oil dripping into you, and be aware of a gentle glow coming from it... Be aware of the cleansing property of this oil...gently cleaning the inside of you... Imagine what it would feel like if you could actually feel it flowing into your body... Maybe part of your feet will feel different...perhaps your toes will start to tingle...or feel warm or just really relaxed... Allow them to feel as comfortable as you choose."

Concentrate on each part of your body in turn, progressing from one end to the other, as in this example: toes, feet, calf muscles, knees, thighs, waist/buttocks, stomach muscles, chest and internal organs, shoulders, arms, hands, fingers, neck, head. Extra attention can be placed on taking the relaxation deeper by going into finer detail from the shoulders up, e.g.:

"There is often a tension in our shoulders that we aren't aware of... Allow the muscles to soften as the warm oil flows gently in, glowing, and cleaning out the effects of stress... Notice how it flows into each fibre of muscle, into the nerves, deep into the bones... Now feel it flowing up the arteries and veins into the neck. Relaxing the muscles even more... Notice how each of the tiny muscles in the face just droops and relaxes...as if on the edge of sleep...the cheek muscles...the jaw...around the lips and around the eyes...across the brow."

Below is a full progressive relaxation script. Remember when you do your recording to speak softly and calmly, as this will help you to relax! In the next chapter I will explain the hypnotic language in greater detail.

"I want you now to draw all of your attention down in to your feet... I want you to notice how they feel... I want you to notice if they feel warm or cold...or maybe just right... As you begin just to wiggle your toes...you just...notice the texture of your socks...and the feeling of your feet against the soles of your shoes or against the floor... Notice how comfortable your feet feel...and just begin to notice how comfortable they could feel if only you wanted them to... Imagine what it would feel like if warm relaxing oil were flowing through them... Imagine if you could see inside your body as if it were transparent... Seeing the oil dripping into you... Noticing a warm glow coming from it...as it just trickles down to your feet...maybe your feet will start to feel different or your toes start to tingle...or maybe they feel warm or just really relaxed...just allow them to feel as comfortable as you choose now... And now that you can imagine this relaxing feeling...in your own time...now...just allow it to creep up into your ankles... As the level of this imaginary oil starts to rise in your body it just goes higher and higher and higher... And with each muscle that it comes into contact with...it just relaxes...unties all the knots and soothes all the stress and tension in the muscle...and relaxes it so deeply...so very deeply... Again in you own time...now...just allow this wonderful feeling to just

travel up into your calves... Just allow your calves to become just as comfortable as you would like them to be... As you imagine that warm, glowing soothing oily liquid just travelling up to your knees...now... Allowing you to relax even deeper as it soothes all your joints and your muscles.... And now as it begins to travel up into your thighs and your...hips...your...buttocks...just allow each and every muscle to just drift and float...and become so very heavy as they begin to relax...deeper...and deeper...and deeper...and deeper... And now as you allow the level of this oil to just rise up and enter your tummy and lower back... It just begins to cleanse all the stress and tension from this area... It just allows you to feel calm and relaxed... This is a place where we tend to hold a lot of emotions...just be prepared to let that emotion go now...as this oil just begins to cleanse deeper and deeper...deeper...deeper...and deeper still... And when you are ready, just take a nice deep breath in...and you inhale all the peace and...beauty and....relaxation that you are experiencing in the lower part of your body now... Your chest just fills with the soothing, relaxing oil and every muscle relaxes as you exhale... And as you exhale release all that stress and tension...and it just disappears from every part of your body...mind and...thought as you just drift and float deeper and deeper relaxed just...take a while to focus on your breathing...and just begin to focus on the rhythm of your breathing as you begin to relax your breathing now... And with every easy breath you take you just go deeper and deeper and deeper relaxed... Feeling more comfortable, more free...and more at peace with yourself... And now you allow this warm glowing feeling to just trickle down into your arms...down to your elbows...down to your wrists...down to your palms...all of the way to the tips...of your fingers... Every part of your arms now...just fills with this soothing relaxing liquid... And you begin to notice that your hands are...heavier...and heavier as you become more and more relaxed... There is often a tension in our shoulders that we aren't aware of... Allow the muscles to soften as the warm oil flows gently in... glowing and cleaning out the effects of stress... Notice how it flows into each fibre of muscle...into the nerves...deep into the bones... Now feel it flowing up the arteries and veins into the neck... Relaxing the muscles even more... Notice how each of the tiny muscles in the face just droop and relax...as if on the edge of sleep...the cheek muscles...the jaw...around the lips and around the eyes... across the brow... And now I would like you to bring all of you attention on your eyes... I would like you to build in your imagination a picture of all of the thousands of tiny little muscles that allow your eyes to open...and to close...and to feel so heavy and tired...when you're at the end of a hard...long...tiresome day... I want you to begin to focus on these muscles now...and as you do...I want you to imagine...that you are cleansing and washing them with this relaxing...flowing...warm oil... And as this oil washes over these muscles...it just allows them to relax so heavy...so deeply...feeling tired...relaxed...and what I would like you to do is to imagine that your eyes are becoming so heavily relaxed...that even if you could be bothered...you just wouldn't be able to even open them... I want you to relax them that deeply for me now... As you just begin to drift and float...drift and float into total relaxation."

Deepeners

After listening to the induction you will more than likely be experiencing some level of light trance. The next step is to take this trance to a deeper state; to do this we use what we call a deepener. A deepener is a suggestion that we give in hypnosis in order to deepen a trance. I have listed here four of my favourite deepeners. All of them tell us a story that gets our mind visualising something. Within them there are suggestions that will help you to feel relaxed, heavy and floaty, etc. The intent of these deepeners is not for you to get so deep that you get to what we call somnambulism, which is a very deep level of trance. Somnambulism is not that useful in therapy, however it is a good state to visit while in hypnosis as it is so beautifully relaxing. The other good thing about a deepener is that you are telling yourself the story, albeit through your recording. You are guiding yourself where you want to go, not just going with the flow and hoping for the best. I want you to use your imagination to the full while using these deepeners to entertain your conscious mind so that the suggestions can seep through to your subconscious in order to assist you in relaxing. You will notice there are a lot of what I call "heavy" words, such as:

- Deep, Down, Fall, Lower
- Tied, Lethargic, Heavy

You will also notice some "light" words, such as:

- Drift, Drifting, Floating

The lift

Here is a deepener that involves getting into a lift and becoming more relaxed as it starts to descend to the basement where there is a really relaxing place for you.

"Just as you are enjoying this beautiful rest...I want you to imagine that you are on the tenth floor of a large building... And you are standing in front of the lift...waiting to descend to the basement...as in the basement is a relaxing room...there will be nice big soft chairs...there will be a beautifully relaxing atmosphere... Now I want you to imagine that you can see the lift doors opening slowly in front of you now... And when you are ready you can just step into the lift... You can find the buttons on the wall and press B for basement... And in a moment I'm going to count from ten to one and with each descending number the lift will go down to the next floor...and as the lift goes down to the next floor...you're going to find yourself becoming more and more deeply relaxed...with every floor that you pass...your body is feeling more and more comfortable...more and more at peace...more and more

relaxed... Your mind will just be focused on going to this...special room...where you can relax even more...even deeper than you are at the moment... So as you are in the lift now... You can start to imagine the buttons there on the wall... You can begin to imagine the colour and the texture of the walls... Notice what the doors are made of...notice how big or small the lift is...when you are ready...lift your hand up to the button and press B...and wait for the lift to descend... Ten...deeper and deeper now...nine...drifting and floating...deeper and deeper and deeper relaxed...eight...you begin to notice how very comfortable your body is beginning to feel and just how deeply relaxed you are...seven...six...five...getting very close to the relaxing room now...four...three...two...one... Now you go on to the ground floor... And in a moment I will say the letter B and when I do the doors will open and you will have arrived...and will be able to step into this peaceful space... You can just flop into one of the chairs and relax deeper and deeper...B"

Pebbles

I love to use this deepener myself. I find it so relaxing and I find it easy to go into a nice level of trance gently and peacefully.

"I want you to imagine that you are standing...on the edge of a large...beautiful and wonderful lake... And as you are standing there...admiring the view...noticing the

atmosphere around you...you pause and just take in...all of its beauty... Just imagine that this beautiful scene helps you to relax and feel comfortable...just sitting there and...taking the time to...just look around...you notice that down by your feet there are ten...smooth pebbles...just right for skimming on the surface of the lake... And in a moment I am going to count...from ten to one...and with each descending number...you're just going to skim the stones...one by one...on this beautiful lake...watching them bounce...across the rippling surface...and every time they bounce...it's almost like it sends ripples of relaxation through your body...and then when I say the next number you take the next pebble and start skimming it across the lake... And relaxing more and more every time that it bounces... Until I get to the number one... This is when you will throw your last pebble... At this time you will just feel that you can't be bothered to play anymore...that you will just be so...beautifully...deeply relaxed...that you would just maybe want to sit there...and enjoy...enjoy the views...as you begin to relax deeper and deeper now... Ten...relaxing deeper and deeper with every bounce...nine...just watching it glide along...eight...seven...six...five...four...three...two... And now on your last pebble...one...as you just sit back...let go and enjoy...watching the last of the ripples...just beginning to fade into the surface of the lake."

Stairs

This deepener seems to be an old favourite among hypnotists and hypnotherapists and certainly if you have ever visited one, you are more than likely to have heard it before! I'm not sure who originally created it, but here is my interpretation of it.

"Ok now I would like you to imagine a beautiful staircase leading down with ten steps... Now I want you to make this staircase your own... You can imagine in to be made from any material you wish...it could be glass...wood or even metal... I want you to make it your own... I want you to make it beautiful... I want you to picture that beautiful special staircase...leading...down...in front of you now... And it is leading down with ten steps... And it's leading to a special place for you... Now I want you to begin to imagine this special place... It could be any place you choose...a mountain...a stream...a beach or maybe just back here where you are at the moment...just somewhere where you can be alone...where you can be comfortable...and relax deeper and deeper... In a moment I am going to count from ten to one...and with each descending number...you're going to feel more relaxed...more at peace...in fact with each descending number you're going to become ten times more deeply relaxed... Ten times more deeply relaxed than you are at the moment... And when I get to one...you will be able to step into that beautiful special place... You're going to be able to experience everything it has to offer...but

most of all you will be so deeply relaxed... Ten...deeper and deeper now...nine...drifting and floating...deeper and deeper and deeper relaxed...eight...you begin to notice how very comfortable your body is beginning to feel and just how deeply relaxed you are...seven...six...deeper and deeper...five...four...three...two...one... You are now in your special place...just relax and enjoy... Take a few moments just to explore this beautiful place."

Ruler

This is a good one to learn for the future. It will help you easily take control of your own relaxation. This is one that I give to people attending my courses as homework.

"Ok I would like you to imagine a ruler in front of you...a meter stick...with numbers from zero to one hundred... Now I want you to imagine that this stick is made out of what ever you wish it to be... You may choose for it to be made from plastic...wood...or maybe even metal... I want you to notice the numbers on it... Notice whether they are in a modern font or maybe in an old-fashioned styled font... Now you see this ruler is very special...because this ruler measures your relaxation... I want you in your mind now just to stand it up on its end with zero at the top and one hundred...way down there at the bottom... And in your own time...I want you to glide your eyes down the ruler and find your true level of relaxation... Remembering that zero is not being relaxed at all and one hundred is being even more

relaxed than you have ever been before... Just take a few moments to find your true level of relaxation on the ruler now...and when you have that reading...I just wonder if you would be able to...imagine going even deeper...going even deeper down to...a different number...a number that would mean you are feeling more relaxed... Now maybe this could be realistic by making it just the next number along on the ruler...or maybe you could move it right along by ten or even twenty numbers...but sure enough as you just set this goal now...and just start to imagine what it would feel like to feel that comfortable to feel your body relaxing more and more with each breath that you take... And as you use your powerful imagination to believe that your body is becoming more relaxed...you find yourself becoming deeper...and deeper...and deeper relaxed...down the ruler to a nice peaceful and gentle state... And I want you to just in your own time...now...start setting goals...in the future...further down your ruler...goals to relax more deeply...goals to get to one hundred on the ruler... Just taking your time now... Just to go deeper and deeper and deeper relaxed... As with this method you can start to take control of your own relaxation by just imagining that you are there...and when you imagine...you surely will become that deeply relaxed...as you just allow this exercise to occupy your mind now...just relaxing deeper and deeper with every number that you pass... Just feeling so comfortable and relaxed now...just drifting and floating..."

Coming up

As an ending to your recording, count yourself back to full alertness. Suggest to yourself that when you leave hypnosis you will feel revitalised and rejuvenated. Test that you are fully awake and alert, and then take pleasure in the rest of your day! Below is a "coming up" script that you can use.

"In a moment...I'm going to count from one to ten... And when I do...with each ascending number that you hear...you are going to feel more refreshed...more rejuvenated...and...as you feel more refreshed and more rejuvenated...all of the negative suggestions that you have been given...about feeling...heavy...tired...lethargic...will fade and be removed... And all of the positive suggestions will just be magnified... When I get to ten you will open your eyes and feel as though you have had a long...beautiful rest...full of energy...one...coming up now...two...feeling more and more alert...three...four...five...more and more awake...six...seven...eight...nine....open your eyes and ten....feel great!"

Dealing with Issues and Building Effective Suggestions

"We are what we think. All that we are arises with our thoughts. With our thoughts, we make the world."

Buddha (544 BC - 624 BC)

Dealing with Issues and Building Effective Suggestions

In many areas of our lives we are so involved in what we don't want and then once in a blue moon constructively think about what we actually do want. For instance, have you ever thought, "It would be so nice not to have to worry about those bills and my dwindling bank balance", or, "I hate that car, it never starts in the morning"? Well this is so natural for most of us; I know I used to do it like this!

By setting and achieving goals we are able to turn these thoughts around and reframe them; for instance, you could say, "I am going to earn substantial amounts of money". This way with a bit of planning you will never have to worry about the bills again! We can turn these into realistic outcomes by first believing in them and then making them well formed. When creating these well-formed outcomes, remember that you set the limit on what is impossible! Take some time now, to have a think and to make a list of things that you don't want in your life, things that really tend to irritate you! For example,

- *"I hate my job; I wish I didn't work there anymore!"*
- *"I don't want them to treat me like that again!"*

You can list them on a separate sheet.

As I mentioned earlier in the book, everything that we do starts with a thought. What I would like you to do now, is to spend sometime collecting your thoughts regarding these things in your life that you have decided that you don't want. I want you to start coming up with some reasons exactly why you don't want them or need them. I want you to find the best outcome that would counterbalance the situation and get rid of what you do not want. For instance, if you have ever had money difficulties or maybe are experiencing money difficulties at the moment, your point will more than likely be, "I don't want to have to go through life with no cash, no money, having to worry about the bills or whether ends are going to meet." Well with a bit of thinking you will be able to come up with the ideas that will, if they happen, change your life. You could develop the outcomes that will make your life comfortable and enjoyable and – the best thing – you will never have to feel like this again.

Over the years in the media I have heard stories of people who have won the lottery, getting millions of pounds, only to end up less happy than before. With the exercise that we are about to do, this has no chance of happening; the reason being that I am not going to show you how to win the lottery. Trust me – if I knew how to do this I would be off on some nice exotic beach somewhere sipping cocktails! However, what I will do is teach you techniques that could change your life for the better, that could even drive you in time to make ridiculous amounts of cash. The whole technique starts with a thought. I know that this technique works as it has proved its effectiveness over thousands of years. All success uses this technique, starting with a single thought, progressing with it into an ambition and then reaching the goal. Some people use this technique subconsciously and achieve only mediocre results, and the rest? Well, they take it, maximise it and manipulate it to get the life that they always wanted. This is a completely natural technique that we all practice on a daily basis. What I want you to do is understand it and use it as it should be used!

If by now you are thinking to yourself, "I'm never going to achieve the sorts of things that Richard is saying I can achieve." Then sadly you are right! To be honest with you, the reason you think that it is never going to happen, is because you THINK it is never going to happen! Read these wise words:

"Whether you believe you can do a thing or not, you are right."

Henry Ford (1863 – 1947)

I want to just quickly go over a point that I made in a previous chapter. Think of people, famous people or people around you, who are successful. Now the only difference between them and someone that is not a success is that they thought, dreamt and made the outcome that they wanted. So it's not just the thought – but this is where it starts. I want you to think of a seed. The seed is a metaphor for your thought. When we think about seeds they all look the same, small, insignificant; some could even be dismissed as specks of dirt. However I want you to believe that this seed is strong, even though it's small. It's strong because it is well formed and it has you to look after it. If you choose to put it in the soil and look after it, then it will grow into a mighty oak, far bigger than the original seed. In the same way, if you allow your thoughts to grow into ambitions you too can achieve success far greater than your original thought.

Going back to your list – as you continue to reframe all the points you made about the things that you don't want, you will be able to come up with a whole list of things that you do want in life. Now that you know what you want you can put your foot on the first rung of the ladder. These are your seeds and your dreams, allow them to grow.

You have probably noticed that I have mentioned "well-formed outcomes" regularly, so let me explain exactly what they are. First let's start with the "outcome" bit. Your outcome is what you want to happen, it's your dream. For instance, your dream may be to have a four-bedroom house in the affluent part of town, a new car, nice spouse and children. This may be your idea of success; if it is, then this would be your outcome. Next let's look at how you would make it "well formed." In order to make your outcomes well formed what I would like you to do is to take some sheets of paper and write a different outcome from your list at the top of each one. Working with one at a time, what I would like you to do is to list the main things that you would need to achieve in order to accomplish this outcome. I will take the outcome that I used before as an illustration to show you the next step. Part of the outcome was to have a new car; however, if you have never learnt to drive, this will have to be one of your main things that you would need to put on your list along with getting the finances to buy and maintain your new car. Then we can take these goals and split them down again. To get the finances you may need to get a better job, a promotion or a pay rise. To get this you may need to take some additional training. To do this you will have to source that training and to do this, you could visit the library. So put basically, getting your new car could all start with something as simple as visiting the library. So just to review, you need to make up loads of sub goals or smaller goals. These sub goals are more achievable and when we achieve them all, we get the outcome that we both wanted and planned. You will be very surprised to find out how simple it becomes to get what you want, when you want it. You will know exactly what direction you need to go in to get everything that you desire. It really is this simple: You can achieve your goals with perfect clarity, knowing exactly where you are going, what you will be doing and, most of all, what you will be achieving. Remember to still be flexible as these outcomes could change at any time due to external factors. This is fine, as we can just change the route and still end up at the same destination.

You're probably wondering why you picked up a book on hypnosis, but instead you are getting a life coaching lesson. Well it is as simple as this. I think they both compliment each other very well and I use this technique with clients on a daily basis to help them realise their goals. This chapter is all about forming suggestions. In order to use suggestion hypnosis you need to know what to suggest. With suggestion hypnosis you can be specific. It's as simple as giving the suggestion and getting the result that you require. Unfortunately I can't put you in hypnosis and say that you will be a millionaire and that magically a wedge of cash will be found in your pocket. However, what I can do is work with you on the smaller goals to affect the bigger picture. This is what we have already started to do.

One of my recent well-formed outcomes is this book, so if you're now reading this then I guess that I was successful. However, I used this same technique and planned everything down to the last detail, so that I knew I would pull it off! From my goals I made suggestions about achieving certain things in set amounts of time. So I would like you to do the same and create suggestions from your sub goals, find areas that you may struggle with and make suggestions to compensate. You will be able to put these suggestions into your own script to use in your hypnosis sessions. Work with these suggestions regularly until you notice improvement and you have accomplished what you wanted to do.

Creating suggestions

To create suggestions is really very simple, to my mind there is really only one rule. That is to be positive, word your suggestion with optimism. Don't say "I want to be more confident", but "I AM more confident", or "I will be more confident" and "day by day I am becoming more and more confident". Say it like it's a fact, like it has already happened. Once you have done your script you can include it between the Induction and coming up scripts that I gave you earlier in the book. Also in the following chapters there are scripts to help people with issues such as smoking, slimming, stress, phobias and confidence. Looking at those will give you an insight into how to word your script.

Hypnotic language

As I mentioned in the Inductions chapter, in hypnosis more often than not, the way we say things aids relaxation more than the words themselves. Say something in a relaxing manner, like, "I want to go and take a nice long, hot bath and relax"; now say the same thing in an aggressive manner. See what I mean? Try to experiment with talking in a slow, deep, monotonous voice. You will probably find this really funny at first, especially when you hear yourself on your recording. The best advice that I could give you is try to experiment with friends or family.

With this chapter you have learnt so much. You have leant to realise exactly what you want in life and exactly how to go out and get it. You have also learnt how to put your suggestions together into a script, and finally the hypnotic language itself.

What I want you to do now, is to come up with those scripts that will help you to achieve all you want in life. I wish you all the success and happiness on this journey – good luck.

Uses of Hypnosis for Effective Change

"The crème de la crème of self-empowerment is hypnosis!"

Olf Stoiber, November 2004

Uses of Hypnosis for Effective Change

The subconscious mind is the filing cabinet that keeps all the information regarding who we are. Everything that happens to us in life is recorded here, however big or small. The information that this filing system holds makes up our character and personality.

What I want you to do is to visualise that your mind contains three parts and each of these three parts has a different function and task to complete, as described below.

Your conscious mind

This is the area of the mind where we use our logic. We weigh up pros and cons in order to make decisions. It is also the platform where our subconscious mind presents thoughts and ideas, for instance have you ever had a thought just pop into your head from what seems like nowhere? If your answer is yes then this is what I mean by an unconscious thought popping into your conscious platform. This is what happens when you are with someone and you almost know what they are going to say next. This happens because you are in rapport with that person and when we are in rapport we begin to communicate subconsciously as well as verbally. This, I understand, may seem a little strange; however, it is just science at the end of the day.

Your filter

Our filter is our beliefs and our ethics; it's where we distort information so that it becomes our interpretation of the world. For instance, if you had a phobia of flying (a belief) and you had just won a holiday for two in Hawaii, your interpretation of the situation would be different from that of, say, someone who loved to fly!

Your subconscious mind

Well, I liken this to an oil painting: Imagine that when you are born you are a blank canvas, with just faint pencil lines marking out your genetics and DNA. Every minute from now on your painting starts to take shape. Everything you see, hear and experience is recorded on your canvas. And slowly and surely you grew into the masterpiece you are today!

We include in our painting our "learnt behaviours"; these are behaviours and automatic responses that we teach and train ourselves over time. They could be anything from smoking to, say, shaking uncontrollably with nerves.

Learnt Behaviours

Let's stick with smoking to explain learnt behaviours in more detail. Smoking is a really common learnt behaviour and if you do not smoke, you more than likely know someone who does. Smoking is not a logical thing to do.

Most people seem to take up the habit because they want to fit into their community – for instance, school children. I frequently see young people in the streets, no older than thirteen or fourteen, smoking. When I see these same people coming into my office as adults, I always ask them why they started to smoke. Nine times out of ten I will be given the answer, "I wanted to fit in and look cool!" and "I wanted to feel comfortable with the guys around me and do what they were doing!" When I ask then about their first cigarette it seems to bring a cringe on their face as they just go back in their mind and remember the first cigarette they inhaled. In fact that first cigarette seemed to make it even more illogical for them to smoke, given that they coughed and spluttered and felt quite ill afterwards. In fact, if they wanted to remain a smoker, at this point they would need to take some action. And this can even involve lying to oneself. They tell themselves that "it doesn't taste so bad" and of course the more that they smoke the more their body allows them to get used to it. They get used to the horrible fumes and the toxic chemicals going into their lungs and at this point the learnt behaviour is born!

Not all learnt behaviours are negative; in fact, quite the opposite. Learnt behaviours are normally excellent in helping you in your everyday life. On the next page is the sequence of events that we go through in order to create a learnt behaviour:

- Make a decision ("I want to learn to drive")
- Take action
- Repetitively take action (keep doing the same thing over and over)
- Get used to and comfortable with the action

We go through this process to get used to things, and by doing this our subconscious mind starts to expect these things to happen. At this point it will become a habit, aka a learnt behaviour. Take a moment to think of all the things that you have learnt over the years that maybe were a little bit tricky at first, but now are second nature – even learning to like something such as a piece of clothing, a car or a type of food. In the next section I will be covering automatic responses, which are not separate from learnt behaviours. Automatic responses are the "side-effects" of our learnt behaviours; I will cover this more in the next section.

Automatic Responses

In this section of the chapter we will be looking into automatic responses. As I said previously these are the "side-effects" to learnt behaviours. Still using smokers as our example, let's go a bit deeper and actually find out what these responses are. The majority of smokers that I see, who tell me how they have made this behaviour, also tell me of times they have had a cigarette, when friends or family would interrupt them and say, "You've just put one out!" They then share with me their amazement and disappointment that they have let this habit get so uncontrollable. When I used to smoke this happened to me regularly. Sometimes without even thinking I would grab for my cigarette packet and have one with little control over myself at all.

The question is what actually made me have a cigarette, as I didn't make the decision consciously. It was almost like I was on autopilot. Simply my subconscious mind expected me to smoke, as this is what I was telling it by constantly repeating the behaviour, so it initiated the process as an automatic response. Sometimes it is blindingly obvious why this automatic response happens. A smoker will regularly suggest that they smoke to relieve stress. Even though this is physically not true, psychologically there are arguments to suggest that it is, because there is a comforting aspect in doing something you do regularly. In certain times of severe or instantly induced stress, smokers can be almost uncontrollably driven to pick up their cigarette packet and light up.

Another example of automatic response is when we are driving, the tempo of the engine changes and we automatically know at this point to change gear. We do not logically think about it, it just happens, we respond subconsciously and do it. There are thousands of things that we do in our everyday lives that we do subconsciously and automatically. Certain actions are not as calculated consciously as we think. Why, as you are sitting there reading this book your body and your mind are achieving thousands of different things in order to protect you. For instance, your heart is beating, your lungs are breathing and you are subconsciously aware of your surroundings so that if something happens externally, you would be able to react and make yourself safe. If someone chucked a ball at you, you would automatically put your hand up, in order to stop this ball hitting you in the face. So again, just like learnt behaviours, these automatic responses have a positive purpose and also a negative purpose.

You are probably wondering why we are covering such deep psychological issues in a self-help book about hypnosis. Well I'll tell you, understanding is the first step to achieving; for example, imagine a CEO of a large failing company on his first day in the position. The first thing in order to achieve amazing results in turning this company around, is that he must first get to know how the business works. This is exactly the same for us: Even though we haven't just inhabited our bodies, in fact we have been here since we were born, we still need to know how and why things happen. We need to find out the way we build behaviours and why we do what we do. In understanding this, we complete the first steps of change!

Using hypnosis to design and build our lives

Now we are going to look at how hypnosis can help us to deal with these unwanted behaviours and responses and create new ones in order to help us achieve exceptional results in our lives. In the introduction of this book I included a verse that I have on my desk; I will remind you of what it says,

"Believe in Yourself:
You are your greatest asset, there's nothing that you can't do.

No one can keep you from dreaming; only you can make them come true.

What you achieve is determined by the desire you possess.

There is no better feeling than the feeling of success.

Believe in who you are and what you do.
Don't leave things up to fate, it's strictly down to you."

Author Unknown

Now you have an option, you can either carry on with life – just pottering on, allowing fate to take its course – or on the other hand, now that you understand how and why things happen, you could start to change your life and become what you have always wished to be. You can achieve extraordinary results! The information that I have given you in this book is nearly all directed to internal change or self change, but when you start to have success from these changes you will begin to notice that you will also receive external success. Success will breed success, people will respect you for what you have achieved, but most of all you will decide how you want to live life.

Hypnosis will help you by planting suggestions in the subconscious mind so that it is not necessary to keep repeating the behaviour as much as you would normally have to. It makes the results that we wish to achieve far more accelerated. Instead of going through the natural process we are actually going through a design and building process where we decide how fast we want to learn and how fast we want to see results. Take all of the ideas and information that you have learnt while reading this book and come up with suggestions in order to counterbalance your learnt behaviours and responses. In the next chapter there are some suggestion scripts for you to use in certain aspects of your life; they include smoking, slimming, stress, phobias, confidence and public speaking. There are probably other issues that you may wish to deal with, so just take these scripts and use them as ideas to make your own. Merge them together and add your suggestions, play about to see what works best for you. To build your own suggestions refer back to the previous chapter. Most of all, realise that you now have the power and the knowledge to make your life exactly what you want. Before you move on, just take a few moments to dream, to dream about what you are going to achieve tomorrow, what you are going to change by next week and about what amazing goals you are going to be achieving in the years to come! Embrace and enjoy this time in your life as you are on a journey of discovery and fulfilment.

Scripts for Specific Issues

"You must be the change you wish to see in the world."

Mahatma Gandhi (1869 – 1948)

Scripts for Specific Issues

Smoking

Recent studies completed here in the United Kingdom, suggest that most smokers have the desire to quit the habit. It seems like every time I watch the television at home, there is a government-sponsored advertisement about giving up smoking which mentions all the ill effects that you'll suffer if you don't.

With the uptake in people wanting to give up smoking there is also an uptake in the weird to wonderful ways to give up. They now include nicotine replacement, group therapy, acupuncture, and much more. All in all, there are loads of different ways in both medicine and complementary therapy to help you attempt to quit.

Hypnosis is different, as shown in a study compiled by Frank Schmidt and research student Chockalingam Viswesvaran of the University of Iowa. Hypnosis is one of the most successful ways to stop smoking and, most importantly, to stay stopped. The reason that I believe hypnosis can boast this success is that it deals directly with the way that we make our thoughts. I'm not going to go over it too much, as it was covered earlier in the book; however, what I will say is that smoking is a "learnt behaviour" and also an "automatic response", a habit. Now take your mind back to the first cigarette that you smoked, for example. I explained in the beginning of the book, about driving on your first driving lesson and how difficult it was to do. It was probably exactly the same with your first cigarette. I can remember mine, as I used to be a smoker until I gave up with self-hypnosis. With my first cigarette I coughed, spluttered and felt really ill afterwards, but sure day by day I thought that it made me look good, it made me look cool. It gave me something to have in common with the other smokers at my school. I spent my spare time getting used to the smell, getting used to the taste, getting used to that suffocating feeling as your lungs just fill with that toxic gas. This is how I learnt to smoke and in a week or two I was an expert, even reaching for my packet and having what I refer to as subconscious cigarettes. Friends would say, "You have just put one out!" From here on in I enjoyed most if not all of them.

Looking back now, the reasons why I gave up seem a bit strange. You know, when I sit there in my office every day and hear why clients want to give up, it usually comes down to health, their future, or finances. You know it's something stupid like £150,000 over a lifetime that a twenty-a-day smoker would smoke their way through. However, I didn't want to give up for any of these reasons. The reason that I gave up was because I was becoming a hypnotherapist! I had sent my application off to the school, I had paid my fees and the start of the course was getting closer and closer. I thought, "I can't walk into the classroom being a smoker". I thought that it would be hypocritical, me wanting to help people give up smoking. I was even being a little naive at the time, thinking that I could learn to make someone give up, which I now say is impossible as all hypnosis is self-hypnosis. I suppose I felt there was a social pressure that really didn't exist, just like I felt when I wanted to take up smoking in the first place. You know I thought that I would be expected not to smoke, and when I got to school I expected to be in a room of non-smokers who were against smoking. Well, this never turned out to be the case; however, at the end of the day I am glad I'm now free of the habit.

So if you want to give up smoking, this is the chapter in the book for you. Up until now you have learnt how to induce a trance, how to deepen that trance and how to safely and effectively bring yourself out of a trance. Set here below is a script for you to use to aid yourself to give up smoking. You will need to insert this script into the full script at the end of this chapter. Once you have made your recording, listen to it as much as possible and at least once a day. The more you use it the faster the results will be.

With giving up smoking there are certain physical side-effects to look out for. This is because you have a physical addiction to the drug nicotine. When this chemical stops going into your body, you physically crave it. Once all the nicotine has left your body, this addiction will no longer be an issue. It takes roughly 3-4 days for this drug to be cleared out of your system naturally. Nicotine has been compared to (Class A) narcotics in relation to the speed that one can get addicted; however, the withdrawal effects are of no comparison! You can help the nicotine to leave your system faster by drinking more water, as it is deposited in your urine.

Personally I wish you the best of luck on this journey; it's something that I have had to do myself and I hope that you have the same success I had. So make your recording, sit back and enjoy your new life!

Stop Smoking Script

"And as you continue to relax...and continue to go deeper and deeper...thoughts will naturally begin to pop into your mind...about being a non-smoker... You have chosen to be a non-smoker...and that feels great for you... Now...as you just think about your decision...and how it is going to impact positively on your life... As you just take a nice deep breath now...and exhale...you notice that your body is feeling comfortable and relaxed... You notice that to relax your body you don't need...any drugs...any vices...you can simply relax...by taking some nice deep breaths... As you continue to breathe in and out...your body will begin to feel so much healthier...with every breath that you take... Now...you have made it your goal...your outcome...to be a non-smoker...and this goal in your life will be a milestone... By achieving this you will be achieving so much more... Just think about the financial benefits...the money that you are going to save by next year... It will like having a substantial pay rise...Just begin to wonder what you can do with having

these extra funds... It is your decision to be a non-smoker and you feel great having made that decision... And as you begin to think about the benefits to your everyday health...begin to think about the wheezing and the coughing disappearing...and begin to visualise your chest clearing of all alien chemicals...just visualise the process that you are now about to go through in regaining yourself to full health... Your body will start to repair all the damage and return you to full health...your body will begin going through a natural process of healing itself and become fitter and stronger... You are a non-smoker and that's your decision and that feels great...this is the way that you have chosen to go...and for this reason...you are going to make it a success... You have consciously chosen...logically...that smoking is not for you and you have consciously chosen that you do not wish to do it anymore...and that's fine because...what I want you to do now is to just...allow your mind to go back in the past and I want you to remember all the times in your life that you have experienced success...and surely as you begin to think...loads of scenarios will start to pop into your head regarding things that you have achieved...they may be your school results...they may be about when you learnt to ride a bike as a child...they may be about a job that you got...or getting a promotion...buying a new car or a house... These are all areas that we tend to make successes... So as you can see you are a successful person...and you can make a success of what you desire... You have made a success of your desires so far... And now as you just...notice that...success is one of your attributes...and I want you to bring this attribute into the present and you begin to feel the emotions that are present with this success...begin to feel *that success in your body now...you can maybe feel a warmth in your heart or maybe butterflies in your tummy...as you just begin to experience the emotions of success...and now you just visualise allowing this success...just to...go into the future before you...in order to prepare your journey as a non-smoker... As you keep breathing in...and out...you allow that success...that beautiful feeling...to build in your heart now... This feeling will remain with you long after this trance...long after next week...long after next month...it will remain with you for the rest of your life... You now understand and you now know...that you are...that you wish to be...a non-smoker...and for you this is great... The feeling of knowing now...while you are in this beautifully deep relaxing trance...that you are never going to smoke again...feels wonderful... This is the feeling of success... The success that you have chosen...to achieve... You will find that smoke is unappealing, in fact you will not feel that you are deprived...you will not feel that you will miss...cigarettes or smoking... You will simply quit...and find...it almost effortless... as you just listen to your recordings everyday you will just be building on this success of being a non-smoker... At anytime that you may wish to have a cigarette...you can...but you will choose not to...that is to say that you are not an addict...you are not a smoker who doesn't smoke...you are a non-smoker...it's almost like this part of your life can be taken back in time to restart at the point when you first decided to smoke... Your views will be that of a non-smoker... You choose to make your own views regarding smokers... You will not let others' smoke irritate you at all... And now as you just feel so relaxed...contemplate your success...knowing that when you open your eyes you have chosen to be a non-smoker and a happy non-smoker... Now you have made this recording in order to help yourself... You will find the time...on a daily basis for your development... You will find the time on a daily basis to turn your life into the life that you have chosen... There are twenty-four hours in the day...and in those twenty-four hours you will find enough time to design and to create...through the power of hypnosis...the life that you want...the next time that you choose...to use hypnosis in this manner...you will find that you will go so much more deeper and deeper relaxed...and in fact the next time you choose to do hypnosis you will just slip...so easily into this beautiful...relaxing feeling... Just begin to think of the time that you will be spending in hypnosis tomorrow...just allow that time to pop into your head as you just quickly think about your tasks and your chores that you have to complete tomorrow... When you have thought of this time...this will be the time that you stick to... This is your personal development time...just twenty to thirty minutes or so...that you can sit down and listen to your tape and develop yourself... The time that you are thinking of now will be the time tomorrow that you are going to listen to this tape again..."*

Slimming

Every year, the one thing that tends to amaze me, is that I see similar types of clients at similar times of the year. Dieters are by no means an exception. It seems that most people's new years resolution is to get fit and to lose some weight. So it is not surprising that the United Kingdom's diet industry is worth millions and millions of pounds.

There are so many different types of diets out there, including calorie controlled diets, carbohydrate controlled diets – and I have also heard of one called the cabbage soup diet. There are clubs that you can go along to and get group therapy and weekly weigh-ins, and that have whole support networks. Most women's magazines seem to concentrate almost fixatedly on this particular issue. We are certainly a nation becoming obsessed with the way we look and how much we weigh. This is not such a bad thing, however when we look at government reports, the situation is only seeming to get worse. The question that we need to ask is whether the dieting industry is really as effective as it says it is.

The other problem is that people are so confused with the diets out there. A lot of these diets have become controversial. There have been loads of articles in the newspapers alleging negative side-effects, with even scientists condemning their use. It's no wonder that most people get confused about the subject and don't even know where to start.

The thing that I find really sad is the craze to look right and how more and more people are taking extreme measures in order to shed a few pounds. Increasingly, people these days are opting for surgical intervention. This I believe is unfortunate as many people just put the weight back on.

Let's take a look why these diets don't tend to work. When most of us come up with the idea of going on a diet, whether it be calorie controlled or carbohydrate controlled, we follow it for a few days and then tend to feel deprived – and this is where the problem comes in, because one part of us wants to be successful and lose weight and the other part is craving a chocolate bar. I wouldn't like to deprive myself to get something. If I want to give up something then it's because I want to give it up. If it had been part of my life for so long, say for instance a kebab on a Friday night or fast food on my lunch break in the middle of the day, I understand that I would miss it. I will tell you later how using hypnosis beats deprivation. Of course the other thing with diets is that they are mostly short-term. Sure we get the pounds off fast for a holiday, a wedding or a specific date when we want to look nice. Generally diets are about losing weight in a short period of time. When we reach our goal we tend to think that everything is OK and we just go back to our old eating habits, this is where the yoyo effect comes in. When we put weight back on we go on a diet to take it back off again.

So how can hypnosis help? Well, as explained in the section on smoking and earlier on in the book, hypnosis helps by dealing with learnt behaviours. How we eat is a habit, you've guessed it; a habit is a learnt behaviour. We have taught ourselves to be exactly who we are. Hypnosis is able to go straight into the subconscious mind and change these learnt behaviours by suggestion. This makes it extremely successful. The best thing of all is that you can design and create new responses, new behaviours and a whole new approach to the way that you think about food, the way you use food and the way you enjoy food. And of course on the other hand you can create a whole new approach to the way that you think about exercise. You may wish to have a whole new experience, say playing a sport like football, badminton or squash. Maybe you want to increase the things that you already do like walking or running – or you could even get off the bus one stop early or park further from work and walk in. Hypnosis can help you to create these new mindsets in an easy and fast way. Instead of forcing yourself and depriving yourself of these habits in such extreme ways, you can use hypnosis to go straight to the root of the problem. You can deal directly with the part of your mind where the behaviours are located.

The science behind losing weight is simple. You put fewer calories in and you take more calories out, with the use of exercise. Here is a challenge for you to sit down and come up with your own diet. Plan the way you wish to achieve this, however bear in mind not to set short-term goals, but long-term ones. Lose weight for the long term, not the short term. Changing your life to eat healthier and exercising to get fit will benefit you no end. Remember you should always enjoy everything that you do, and losing weight is no exception!

Slimming Script

"As you just continue to...relax...deeper and deeper...you choose to hear my voice...and be able to focus on it...or maybe you can hear my voice but can't be bothered to focus on it...either is perfectly fine... What I want you to do next is to...relax...now you have decided that your goal for the future in to lose weight...you know in your mind if this goal...that you have set...is short-term or long-term... You know what you will need to do in order to lose this weight... You have made the decision to begin to exercise...you have made the decision to eat...sensibly... You have made the decision to make a success in every part of this...goal... You have been able to sit down and plan... You have been able to desire this outcome and to build it into a well-formed outcome... As you just begin to build a picture in your mind...of the lighter you...the slimmer you...and you notice that this picture looks great... Just imagine wearing what you want... Allow yourself to glow radiantly... This picture in your mind is now set as your goal... You add to your goal a realistic time scale...to achieve this goal... And as you think of all this now...it will become your day of reckoning...this will be the day that you will have achieved...this wonderful...wonderful goal... You have made the decision...to respect and love yourself and your body...from inside out... Even though at the moment you haven't physically reached your goal...mentally you have... Part of your goal is that you want to be content...when you have your new body... You will start to notice a love for your body

starting to build now...a love and respect... This is why you are losing weight...because of the love and respect for yourself... Just take time now to think how life will be so...different without this excess weight... It will be easier to climb stairs...to play sports...losing this weight secures time in your future... As in society we notice that people are getting serious illnesses earlier and earlier in their lives due to being overweight...you now choose for your life to not be like this...and have this problem or issue... The correct amount of food for you will be filling... Maybe in the past you have had issues with linking food to stress...maybe as automatic responses... This will not happen anymore...because you choose for it not to... Foods that are in anyway unhealthy for you or do not fit your diet...will not appeal to you...in any way whatsoever...because you only have one thing on your mind and that is your success... You will begin to enjoy things like fruit... You begin to start experimenting with different foods that maybe you haven't tried before and that are healthy for you and are full of vitamins...minerals...and fibre... You begin to find out more about and learn about food... How to make it tasty... satisfying...and healthy... You begin to think about exercise and not just thinking about it...but actually start to increase your level of exercise... You may choose to do this in a small way or you may wish to have a radical change...you will start to increase on a daily basis...your exercise routine until you have reached your peak... all of these new habits...eating correctly...and exercising properly...will lead to permanent weight loss...they will lead to a new beautiful life for you... Just take a few moments to just contemplate this new wonderful life...you begin to feel so much more positive about this new beautiful experience...you begin to see yourself as an attractive person...with intelligence and creativity...with value and most importantly with love for yourself... These positive feelings begin to grow stronger and stronger on a daily basis...as you become the person that you wish to be and achieve your goal... Now you have made this recording in order to help yourself... You will find the time...on a daily basis for your development... You will find the time on a daily basis to turn your life into the life that you have chosen... There are twenty-four hours in the day...and in those twenty-four hours you will find enough time to design and to create...through the power of hypnosis...the life that you want...the next time that you choose...to use hypnosis in this manner...you will find that you will go so much more deeper and deeper relaxed...and in fact the next time you choose to do hypnosis you will just slip...so easily into this beautiful...relaxing...feeling... Just begin to think of the time that you will be spending in hypnosis tomorrow...just allow that time to pop into your head as you just quickly think about your tasks and your chores that you have to complete tomorrow... When you have thought of this time...this will be the time that you stick to... This is your personal development time... just twenty to thirty minutes or so...that you can sit down and listen to your tape and develop yourself... The time that you are thinking of now will be the time tomorrow that you are going to listen to this tape again..."

Stress

We live today in a society that seems to be fuelled by stress, with so many people suffering the side-effects of the negative responses caused by stress. Nowadays people are working harder, thinking more about their careers rather than themselves. This is where most stress tends to take its toll, in the rat race. People who live hectic lives have less recreational time, less time to relax, less time to enjoy themselves with family and friends. Things just seem to build up, one thing leads to another and stress begins to take over.

Stress management is another exceptionally big industry here in the United Kingdom. Hypnosis is incredibly successful in dealing with stress, as it is able to relax the mind in a matter of seconds. When the mind is more relaxed we can deal with the things that are stressing us with more stability and clarity. Stress tends to occur when our mind clogs up with things like confusion and maybe even fear, fear for the future or even what's just around the corner. This chapter aims to deal with the stress and not the initial issue which caused the stress; sure, once we have managed to deal with the stress the situation that triggered it may still be present, however by dealing with the stress your mind will be clearer and much more effective in dealing with this situation. We have all heard of the saying, "Running around like a headless chicken", which is generally related to people who are stressed. And it is true, people rush around not knowing if they are coming or going. They need to take the time to sit down, and to start dealing with and managing their stress. How can we expect to be successful in our everyday lives externally if we don't take the time to deal with the stuff going on internally?

It is my belief that stress is an extremely important thing to have in your life! It's there for a reason. The reason is to aid us in our motivation. I have really enjoyed writing this book so far; however, it has had its stresses. I set myself deadlines so that I knew that I would be under a certain amount of pressure. I also set certain standards that I needed to achieve in the book; this has put me under a little stress which is good because it has pushed me to get this book in your hands today!

The script that follows is specifically designed to deal with everyday stress. If you are suffering from severe stress or anxiety, then it is really important that you get professional help; whatever the case you should notice that this script will help you a great deal. If you are using this script because you consider yourself to be stressed, then use it regularly. It includes suggestions that build relaxation into your everyday life. Remember that it is important to take time for you. Many people go about their everyday lives not even knowing who they are, they never give themselves the chance to get to know what makes them happy, what makes them sad and what makes them stressed! I find this a truly astonishing point, because I believe that before we can go out and make a success of our lives, we need to know what our tools are and how to use them and also to know whether any of them are in need of fixing or sharpening. The other reason that it is so important to take the time for you, is that the stress we suffer contributes to and sometimes even creates some of the illnesses we can be afflicted with. There are so many types of condition that are said to be stress-related. For instance, heart problems, skin disorders or asthma are all issues that are affected by stress.

In order to deal with stress today there is no need to escape the rat race, no need to make massive changes in your life, but there is a big need to get to know yourself! Get to know what relaxes you, get to know what triggers your stresses, what makes you happy and know exactly what tools you already have in your tool box. Choose not to live like a headless chicken, but to live as a success!

Stress Script

"As you begin to relax deeper and deeper... You have made the decision to get rid of the excess stress in your life... You have made the decision to deal with the things that unsettle you...and cause you stress... You have decided to create a life that is free from all types of negative stress... You have decided to use stress in your life in a positive way by manipulating it and directing it... This type of stress will push you and motivate you to achieve your goals... I want you to become very aware of your body...and your mind now... I want you to begin to create an image...of your body and mind...there in front of you... They need not be two separate images as in life the body and mind are one... The

*body and mind work as one...and in no way can be split...
What I would like you to do is notice in what parts of your
body...stress takes it effect... For instance when some
people get stressed they panic...when they panic their
heart will race...they may get a heavy feeling in their
chest...and their stomach might feel like lead...their mind
could get confused...just build into this image...using
colours...where the stress affects you... You may choose to
visualise...a red colour in your mind to represent the
confusion...you may choose a black colour in your tummy
to represent the heaviness... you may have a brown colour
in your chest to represent the pressure... Just make this
visualisation in your mind...now...using whatever colours
you wish...slowly I want you bring all these colours
together...and I want you to merge them into one
colour...and make it into a ball... As you do this all the
stress in your picture will go to one part of your body...to
form this ball... Now let all of your awareness be focused
on this ball... Just visualise that you are taking it in your
hands...and as you do...it just seems that all the little bits of
stress that are left in your body...just seem to be sapped
out of your body and into this ball...I want you to give this
ball a name...any name you wish...but a name that
represents the way that you feel about this stress... See it
there in front of you...you have no fear of it...as all your
stresses are in there and not in your body... You have
complete control over it... Our imagination controls so
much of what we do and how we feel... During trance your
imagination...is occupied with stories that help your body to
relax... So by making mental imagery...we can achieve
physical responses... As you begin to look at this ball...I
want you to begin to change the colour...and rename it...*

Rename your ball with a name that represents something beautiful and special to you... This could be a place that you go on holiday...it could be your favourite type of car...or maybe a nice animal... Now begin to change the whole appearance of your ball...this may take some time and that's fine... As you begin to imagine the original colour just draining from it and almost becoming white... You can now add your new colour...your new...peaceful...relaxing colour... And then I want you to imagine that this ball has...such energy...such peaceful and relaxing energy... And you can now feel this positive energy going into your hands... As you continue to build these positive emotions...you can wonder what it would feel like if this ball was just made out of pure love... Pure love and relaxation... Just imagine how beautiful it would be... Now that you have been able to build this ball of happiness and...contentment...love...and relaxation...slowly begin to deliver it back into your body now... begin to notice how good it feels...to have that relaxation...that love...and that respect for yourself...just relax more and more now... You have chosen to get rid of the excess stress in your life...and that's fine...that's great with you...and it's already beginning to happen now... You notice how beautifully relaxed you are at the moment...and this relaxation will be anchored into your everyday life... In general you are going to feel more relaxed...more at peace...and more calm with your surroundings... Being more relaxed, you will notice that you have a clearer head...in order to deal with stress head on before it affects you negatively... You will be able to manage stress perfectly...and achieve results that you want to achieve...because stress will no longer be in the way...of you reaching your goals... Stress is no longer a negative factor in your life... It will only be used for positive measures in order to achieve amazing results... As you just relax deeper and deeper now...breathing in perfect relaxation and breathing out all the negativity... Day by day these positive suggestions will begin to grow and the more that you listen to this recording...the more stress-free you will begin to be... Now you have made this recording in order to help yourself... You will find the time...on a daily basis for your development... You will find the time on a daily basis to turn your life into the life that you have chosen... There are twenty-four hours in the day...and in those twenty-four hours you will find enough time to design and to create...through the power of hypnosis...the life that you want...the next time that you choose...to use hypnosis in this manner...you will find that you will go so much more deeper and deeper relaxed...and in fact the next time you choose to do hypnosis you will just slip...so easily into this beautiful...relaxing... feeling... Just begin to think of the time that you will be spending in hypnosis tomorrow...just allow that time to pop into your head as you just quickly think about your tasks and your chores that you have to complete tomorrow... When you have thought of this time...this will be the time that you stick to... This is your personal development time... just twenty to thirty minutes or so...that you can sit down and listen to your tape and develop yourself... The time that you are thinking of now will be the time tomorrow that you are going to listen to this tape again..."

Phobias

This is the part of the chapter where we take a look at phobias. A lot of people tend to get confused about the difference between a fear and a phobia. This is not surprising considering that they are relatively similar and both can have negative emotional effects. To basically explain the differences between them, I will start with fears. It is a little-known fact that fears are actually a good thing to have; they are there to protect us. They stop us from doing stupid things that are going to hurt us. To put it in a comical way I suppose I could say that I am fearful of falling! Now having this fear keeps me safe and protects my life. For instance if I were standing on top of a ten-story building, I would reasonably fear taking the quickest route to the ground floor, which would mean stepping off the edge! Now this is an extreme interpretation, so let's look at some day-to-day fears, such as the fear of touching hot things in case we get burnt. I have a piranha at home and I have a fear of putting my hand in the tank when I'm cleaning or feeding her! The rule is that the majority of fears are just there to protect us, so it wouldn't be good to get rid of them.

On the other hand a phobia is a negative thing. A phobia was probably at one point a fear. Then the fear became irrational. Take children for instance, a large number have a fear of the dark. Now I'm not saying that this is a good thing, however it is understandable because they lack understanding and experience in life, so this would be a rational fear. If this fear follows us into adulthood then it is usually irrational and becomes a phobia. Then it can affect us in many negative ways in areas such as our work, home lives, or even our love lives. Think about it, what if you were scared of the dark now? Imagine that you needed to sleep with the light on, but it irritated your partner because they couldn't sleep. It would put a certain strain on your relationship; this debilitating fear of the dark would be irrational and classed as a phobia.

There are thousands and thousands of different types of phobias. Psychologists and psychiatrists have taken the time to name them all. A fear of open spaces would be agoraphobia, a fear of spiders is arachnophobia, a fear of bald people is peladophobia and a fear of the furs or skins of animals is doraphobia. Knowing the scientific name for your phobia is not necessary, but you will need to do some research and find out about your phobia. You can do this by using your mind as your reference. First of all see whether there is a need to have that phobia. Then check the ecology to see if not having this phobia will affect you negatively in anyway. Once you are sure that life is going to be better after getting rid of this phobia, then you can make it your aim to use the following script to eliminate it.

The reason that I believe hypnosis can boast about its high success rate in eliminating phobias is that it deals with them quickly and efficiently. Most phobias come down to our subconscious mind not understanding fully. It does not understand that a small spider can't hurt us or that it is safer to travel by air than road.

Use the following script as regularly as possible. Your phobia will more than likely not disappear immediately, however keep persisting and you will get results!

Phobias Script

"As you begin to relax deeper and deeper... You have made the decision to deal with your phobia... And this decision is going to...develop you in so many areas of your everyday life... And as you are just here...perfectly relaxed, you can safely think about exactly what it is that...has become an issue for you...now... As you begin to take a positive approach in... thinking about this phobia that has been an issue for some time...you begin to notice a confidence coming from the fact that...you have decided...now...to resolve all issues that allow the negative impacts of this phobia... You will allow yourself to disassociate from the phobia by simply seeing it in a picture in front of you... I want you to build a visualisation of yourself...and this picture will be a representation...of your phobia... You allow this picture to contain all of the aspects of your phobia... As you just take the time...to dissect your feelings and thoughts regarding this issue...and as you begin to notice... just how it affects you...physically and emotionally... You will now allow all of these aspects to become part of this picture...in fact you can load every negative part of this phobia into this picture...and allow them to be interpreted

in your own way... And when you have your picture...just begin to notice the power that you have allowed these feelings to have over you for so long...when you are ready... I would like you to slowly start...draining all of the colour out of the picture...almost allowing the picture...to become black and white...and then begin to allow it to fade... As you are doing this...allow yourself to notice...whether your feelings about this irrational phobia are changing in any way at all... And when you have achieved this just allow this picture to just...shrink...and allow it to get smaller...and smaller...so that it reaches the size of a postage stamp... And when this is done...allow yourself...to relax even deeper and deeper...as you just begin again to just clear your mind...of thought and focus on this small... insignificant...picture... The fact is that it is insignificant... because you are allowing it to be insignificant... And as you just begin to notice how...powerful that can make you feel... just to allow yourself in your imagination by utilising these visualisations...to play with your emotions and the way that you think about things that seemed to determine the way that you feel... And as you continue focusing on this thought...slowly I want you to create a new picture...this new picture will block out the old...insignificant image... that you have decided to control and put in its place...now that it has become an insignificant entity that you want no longer to be a part of you...and your emotions... And now with this new picture...I want you to produce a visualisation that interprets and depicts everything that is...positive... about your new and successful perception of this old phobia...or behaviour... Visualise what sorts of things you can do now that you have chosen for this phobia not to be a part of your life...now that you have taken control...and you have allowed it to become...insignificant...and as you do this...remember...and allow your subconscious mind to remind you...of all of the times in the past that you have made a success in your life...whether it be...at school...or... in your career...or maybe in a relationship...and even though these events are not related...in one sense they are...as you can allow yourself to notice that you are already a successful person...and success is already an attribute that you actually have and use... I want you to allow this attribute to be depicted in this visualisation...I want you to allow this feeling of success to be brought into your current feelings right now...and also to be represented in your picture...now... When you have added all that you feel you need to into your picture...I want you just to revel in the good feelings that this picture portrays... Revel in the feelings and the knowledge that...when this phobia becomes insignificant to you...this is how you are going to feel...successful...in control...and more able to do things that you have not been able to do before...due to this issue... I want you to make the colours brighter...and the sounds louder... I want you to begin to experience the emotions that this successful picture radiates to you... As you begin to notice how good it feels to be free from something that has held you back for so long...I want you to take time to make this a big significant issue... I want you to take time to experience all that it has to offer. I want you to allow these feelings and what you are seeing to reach a summit...a peak... And at this point I want you to step into the picture...and I want you to allow yourself to become a part of this picture... I want the picture to surround you... and I want you to notice how good it feels as you just remain completely relaxed...completely calm...and completely still...just experiencing what life is going to be like...what the new you is going to be like... I want you to just notice how good it feels as you allow this picture day by day to become part of you... Your subconscious mind will just allow your old responses to the phobia to just fade into the distance and allow you to become a strong and powerful individual...you are an individual who can control yourself and allow yourself to take full control over the way you feel about certain situations... As you just continue to relax...you allow all of these positive emotions...all the strength and all the success just to become part of you...as you relax deeper and deeper now...and take some time to revel in this new-found feeling... Noticing that no longer are the negative sides of this phobia a part of you in any way whatsoever... You just continue to relax deeper and deeper...still... Now you have made this recording in order to help yourself... You will find the time...on a daily basis for your development... You will find the time on a daily basis to turn your life into the life that you have chosen... There are twenty-four hours in the day...and in those twenty-four hours you will find enough time to design and to create...through the power of hypnosis...the life that you want...the next time that you choose...to use hypnosis in this manner...you will find that you will go so much more deeper and deeper relaxed...and in fact the next time you choose to do hypnosis you will just slip...so easily into this beautiful...relaxing...feeling... Just begin to think of the time that you will be spending in hypnosis tomorrow...just allow that time to pop into your head as you just quickly think about your tasks and your chores that you have to complete tomorrow... When you have thought of this time...this will be the time that you stick to... This is your personal development time...just twenty to thirty minutes or so...that you can sit down and listen to your tape and develop yourself... The time that you are thinking of now will be the time tomorrow that you are going to listen to this tape again..."

Confidence and public speaking

Surprisingly, a lack of self confidence affects a large number of people. Because it is an issue that affects your everyday life if you suffer from it, I would like to spend a great deal of time in this book covering how hypnosis can help you. Confidence or a lack of it can affect us in so many different ways, from the moderate to the extreme. It can affect us in small groups of people as well as large and it effects us most within. It affects the way we think about ourselves, how we believe in ourselves, and in turn it affects how people believe in us. Once we get into the habit of low self confidence, it seems to be a vicious circle. The negativity that we radiate about ourselves seems to bounce back in feedback from other people. It disrupts our nerves and makes us anxious; it is closely related to and can breed phobias. These can be social phobias, such as agoraphobia and many others. Some people who suffer from lack of self confidence tend to have physical manifestations of the emotions that can be caused by it. They may stutter when they talk, shake, and even blush; and if they are under severe pressure, they may have a panic attack which could lead to blacking out.

This part of the chapter is also dedicated to public speaking, which is another area where people with low self confidence seem to have a lot of difficulty. They may have a fear of things going wrong, forgetting what they are going to say, or blushing; they may also suffer from stress and feel physically ill.

I can remember when I was a teenager, I got up in front of the local church and delivered a talk. It was the first thing like this that I had ever done and there was me talking about God, something that you would probably never catch me doing nowadays. However I had a job to do and I went ahead and did it. I felt terrible from the time I knew I had to do it, while I was actually doing it, and even afterwards. I was self conscious all the way through and my lack of self confidence certainly showed in the physical manifestations of shaking, stuttering and speaking so fast that hardly anyone could understand me. It made me feel physically sick. This was an issue that I carried with me for the rest of my teenage days. In fact it wasn't until I learnt hypnosis that I got around to dealing with it. Nowadays I think nothing of getting up and sharing my opinion with groups of people. It's quite the opposite now to what it used to be; I now have a passion to get up and speak and I really enjoy it. I suppose part of it is due to the fact that when I talk I now find the topic so interesting and fascinating. However most of it comes down to the work that I have had to do in hypnosis that made public speaking a success for me. I realised that even though public speaking is an external thing, everything that was going wrong was actually on the inside. For some reason I had taught myself to be fearful of this situation, mainly because I didn't believe in myself.

So the basic need in dealing with this situation is to start with number one, to start with you! Start with your beliefs, how you feel about yourself and how you value yourself. These are all-important questions that you need to get the answers to, so that you can deal with them. If we score ourselves quite low then we really need to be doing some work on these issues. In a while I am going to give you two scripts. The first has suggestions in it to aid you to get to know yourself better; it will help you increase your inner confidence, increasing how you value yourself, how you think of yourself and how much you believe in yourself.

For the things that bother you, like panicking when speaking to someone or any sort of anxiety attack, then I will refer you back to the previous section on phobias. Mix and match the scripts and come up with your own script. The first script that I am going to give you covers the basics; it includes suggestions regarding how you feel about yourself in general. You should aim to use this script as much as possible, over the coming weeks.

If you have a problem with public speaking then when ready you will be able to use the second script. This script has specific suggestions that aim to deal with issues that may arise while speaking in public. In my career today, I have found that enjoying public speaking has been a great benefit. It has helped me to build my practice and my training schemes no end. You will find that the script contains a large amount of forward pacing; this along with the suggestions should really help you to pull through and deal with this issue. Sit back regularly and dream about giving presentations and talks and everything going absolutely perfectly. This type of forward pacing out of trance will help you no end. I used to imagine myself giving great speeches, great talks, with only the dog sitting in front of me! This sounds a bit crazy, however it helped me to control the way that I wanted to feel. It prepared my subconscious and taught it a new set of responses, showing it how I want to feel when I speak. I learnt that I am not a slave to my emotions and feelings, but that they are slaves to me. I can choose how I want to feel when I get up on the stage. I can choose to feel nervous, anxious, maybe appearing shaky – or I can choose to appear confident, full of knowledge and experienced. I can leave the stage with a sense of achievement.

I really want to wish you well in using both of these scripts and I hope that over time, you find the joy in both everyday life and public speaking that I have been able to find. My tip to you is to just keep going: Keep persisting, and you will make it.

Confidence Script

*"And as you are just continuing to relax there beautifully...
and deeply...I want you to begin to build a picture... A
picture of yourself...standing in front of you now...and in
this picture I want you to notice...how you value...yourself at
the moment...how you believe in yourself at the moment...
Make this picture a representation of exactly how you feel
about yourself...physically and emotionally... I want you to
know that you are in control of this whole situation...in fact
you are in control...now...of your complete existence...you
can choose to decide...feelings...emotions...you can choose
to change aspects...aspects in your life that you feel...hold
you back... Over the coming days your subconscious mind
is going to point you in the direction of development... Your
subconscious mind is going to feed you... with the
confidence... the respect... and the love for yourself... that
you so rightly deserve... and have chosen to now be a part
of your life... As you build this picture in front of you... I want
you to begin to slowly... change its appearance... So many
times in life we look at ourselves and we paste all of our
thoughts and emotions with negativity... so during the
period of this visualisation I want you to allow yourself to...
remove that filter and I want you to allow yourself to see
this picture... in a positive... fun... and happy light... I want
you to allow the negativity to drain out of this picture as you
allow in positive emotions as you build in... strength...
power into this image... As you begin to dream about
exactly who you want to become... allow all of this
information just to sink in and become a part of your
picture... now... Next I want you to allow the emotions... and
the feelings of this picture to just begin to touch you...*

now... so that you can experience the beautiful feeling of... success... power... and strength... And I want you to allow this... emotional exercise to... reach a summit or a peak... I want you to allow these emotions to feel intense in your physical and mental body now... As you just relax deeper and deeper... and as these emotions start to peak and reach their summit... the picture slowly starts to become a part of you now... Your subconscious mind will embrace this picture and it will become...you... Subconsciously your mind will be working for you on a daily basis to make this picture a reality... And as you continue to relax there... deeply...deeply relaxed...you are safe in the knowledge that now you are making the preparation...you are beginning to climb the ladder and you are a step closer to becoming the person you always dreamt you would be... And as you just relax...deeper and deeper...now all of these positive suggestions are going to be magnified into your subconscious mind...as you just enjoy this powerful feeling... Now you have made this recording in order to help yourself... You will find the time...on a daily basis for your development... You will find the time on a daily basis to turn your life into the life that you have chosen... There are twenty-four hours in the day...and in those twenty-four hours you will find enough time to design and to create...through the power of hypnosis...the life that you want...the next time that you choose...to use hypnosis in this manner...you will find that you will go so much more deeper and deeper relaxed...and in fact the next time you choose to do hypnosis you will just slip...so easily into this beautiful...relaxing...feeling... Just begin to think of the time that you will be spending in hypnosis tomorrow...just allow that time to pop into your head as you just quickly think about your tasks and your chores that you have to complete tomorrow... When you have thought of this time...this will be the time that you stick to... This is your personal development time...just twenty to thirty minutes or so...that you can sit down and listen to your tape and develop yourself... The time that you are thinking of now will be the time tomorrow that you are going to listen to this tape again..."

Public Speaking Script

"And as you just continue to...relax deeper and deeper... You have decided now to deal with issues that you have with public speaking...this feeling of being able to take control...feels good to you... You have decided that no longer...do you wish to appear...nervous...shaky... You have decided that in the future...you wish to appear...confident... enthusiastic...competent...successful... You can notice already that all of these aspects are a part of your life... Your subconscious mind will remind you of times in the past...that you have shown your...knowledge on a particular subject... That on a one to one basis...you have been able to give people information and knowledge... And from the past your subconscious mind will show you that you have made successes in many situations... Your subconscious mind will show you times that you have had to be strong... and positive... Your subconscious mind now knows that you are a...competent...positive...and knowledgeable person... The fear that you had of public speaking is in fact irrational...and should not be part of you in any way whatsoever... As you just relax deeper and deeper...now...

you begin to build an image in your mind...of you on a stage...delivering a presentation... You notice that delivering this presentation in your mind feels safe and good... You begin to notice that when you use your imagination to create this visualisation...things feel safe and comfortable...because you can see it at a distance...you can see yourself being on a stage delivering a wonderful presentation... Keep building this picture with everything going fantastically... Allow yourself to oversee you and your audience...as you watch the delivery of your presentation... Build yourself to be a calm...collected presenter...giving good interesting information...really enjoying the job in hand... Allow your audience in your image...to appear happy...content and interested... Notice how you look...notice how smartly you have dressed and how knowledgeable you seem... Notice how passionate you feel...because everything is going so well... Notice how the confidence just seems to...radiate...from you...while on the stage... Begin to notice...the communication of confidence...and knowledge that seems come from you non-verbally and subconsciously... Notice that the audience are engaged intently on what you are saying...waiting for the next piece of tasty information and knowledge that you are going to give them...just allow yourself to sit in the audience...and look at yourself delivering...a great presentation... Notice how interesting and good it feels... Begin to build these feelings up inside yourself...now... Allow...that confidence...that passion...that enthusiasm... that successfulness and that strength to come in and affect you in some way now... When it begins to affect you positively...allow the power of these emotions and feelings to intensify...allow them to become strong and positive in your life now... When you feel that these feelings have reached their summit...their peak...allow yourself to step into the picture and into yourself... Feel how good it feels to be a part of this presentation... Notice that afterwards...you get a massive round of applause and that feels great... In every way possible...now...your subconscious mind will aim to have those responses that you saw in your picture... appear in you when you next give a presentation... No more...stuttering...no more speaking too fast...no more blushing...no more shaking...no more sweating...no more anxiety or panic... Your subconscious mind will give you... strength...power...and enthusiasm...passion...knowledge... competence...and at the end of a presentation...your reward will be that you feel great... Every time that you do a presentation now you will get...stronger and stronger... As you just continue to relax...deeper and deeper...now...while you allow all of these positive suggestions to sink deep into your subconscious and magnify with intensity... Now you have made this recording in order to help yourself... You will find the time...on a daily basis for your development... You will find the time on a daily basis to turn your life into the life that you have chosen... There are twenty-four hours in the day...and in those twenty-four hours you will find enough time to design and to create...through the power of hypnosis...the life that you want...the next time that you choose...to use hypnosis in this manner...you will find that you will go so much more deeper and deeper relaxed...and in fact the next time you choose to do hypnosis you will just slip...so easily into this beautiful...relaxing...feeling... Just begin to think of the time that you will be spending in hypnosis tomorrow...just allow that time to pop into your head as you just quickly think about your tasks and your chores that you have to complete tomorrow... When you have thought of this time...this will be the time that you stick to... This is your personal development time...just twenty to thirty minutes or so...that you can sit down and listen to your tape and develop yourself... The time that you are thinking of now will be the time tomorrow that you are going to listen to this tape again..."

Complete Session Script

Below I have placed a whole script from start to finish, with everything needed apart from the suggestion script. Choose an appropriate suggestion script from the previous sub headings and add it in to the script below.

"I want you now to draw all of your attention down on to your feet... I want you to notice how they feel... I want you to notice if they feel warm or cold...or maybe just right... As you begin just to wiggle your toes...you just...notice the texture of your socks...and the feeling of your feet against the soles of your shoes or against the floor... Notice how comfortable your feet feel...and just begin to notice how comfortable they could feel if only you wanted them to... Imagine what it would feel like if warm relaxing oil were flowing through them... Imagine if you could see inside your body as if it were transparent... Seeing the oil dripping into you... Noticing a warm glow coming from it...as it just trickles down to your feet...maybe your feet will start to feel different or your toes start to tingle...or maybe they feel warm or just really relaxed...just allow them to feel as

comfortable as you choose now... And now that you can imagine this relaxing feeling...in your own time...now...just allow it to creep up into your ankles; as the level of this imaginary oil starts to rise in your body it just goes higher and higher and higher... And with each muscle that it comes into contact with...it just relaxes...unties all the knots and soothes all the stress and tension in the muscle...and relaxes it so deeply...so very deeply... Again in you own time...now...just allow this wonderful feeling to just travel up into your calves... Just allow your calves to become just as comfortable as you would like them to be... As you imagine that warm, glowing soothing oily liquid just travelling up to your knees...now... Allowing you to relax even deeper as it soothes all your joints and your muscles.... And now as it begins to travel up into your thighs and your...hips...your...buttocks...just allow each and every muscle to just drift and float...and become so very heavy as they begin to relax...deeper...and deeper...and deeper...and deeper... And now as you allow the level of this oil to just rise up and enter your tummy and lower back... It just begins to cleanse all the stress and tension from this area... It just allows you to feel calm and relaxed... This is a place where we tend to hold a lot of emotions...just be prepared to let that emotion go now...as this oil just begins to cleanse deeper and deeper...deeper...deeper...and deeper still... And when you are ready, just take a nice deep breath in...and you inhale all the peace and...beauty and....relaxation that you are experiencing in the lower part of your body now... Your *chest just fills with the soothing, relaxing oil and every muscle relaxes as you exhale... And as you exhale release all that stress and tension...and it just disappears from every part of your body...mind and...thought as you just drift and float deeper and deeper relaxed just...take awhile to focus on your breathing...and just begin to focus on the rhythm of your breathing as you begin to relax your breathing now... And with every easy breath you take you just go deeper and deeper and deeper relaxed... Feeling more comfortable, more free...and more at peace with yourself... And now you allow this warm glowing feeling to just trickle down into your arms...down to your elbows...down to your wrists...down to your palms...all of the way to the tips...of your fingers... Every part of your arms now...just fills with this soothing relaxing liquid... And you begin to notice that your hands are...heavier...and heavier as you become more and more relaxed... There is often a tension in our shoulders that we aren't aware of... Allow the muscles to soften as the warm oil flows gently in... glowing and cleaning out the effects of stress... Notice how it flows into each fibre of muscle...into the nerves...deep into the bones... Now feel it flowing up the arteries and veins into the neck... Relaxing the muscles even more... Notice how each of the tiny muscles in the face just droop and relax...as if on the edge of sleep...the cheek muscles...the jaw...around the lips and around the eyes... across the brow... And now I would like you to bring all of your attention to your eyes... I would like you to build in your imagination a picture of all of the thousands of tiny little muscles that allow your eyes to open...and to close...and to feel so heavy and tired...when you're at the end of a hard...long...tiresome day... I want you to begin to focus on these muscles now...and as you do...I want you to imagine...that you are cleansing and washing them with this relaxing...flowing...warm oil... And as this oil washes over these muscles...it just allows them to relax so heavy...so deeply...feeling tired...relaxed...and what I would like you to do is to imagine that your eyes are becoming so heavily relaxed...that even if you could be bothered...you just wouldn't be able to even open them... I want you to relax them that deeply for me now... As you just begin to drift and float...drift and float into total relaxation... Ok, now I would like you to imagine a beautiful staircase leading down with ten steps... Now I want you to make this staircase your own... You can imagine it to be made from any material you wish...it could be glass...wood or even metal... I want you to make it your own... I want you to make it beautiful... I want you to picture that beautiful special staircase...leading...down...in front of you now... And it is leading down with ten steps... And it's leading to a special place for you... Now I want you to begin to imagine this special place...it could be any place you choose...a mountain...a stream...a beach or maybe just back here where you are at the moment...just somewhere where you can be alone...where you can be comfortable...and relax deeper and deeper... In a moment I am going to count from ten to one...and with each descending number...you're going to feel more relaxed...more at peace...in fact with each descending number you're going to become ten times more deeply relaxed... Ten times more deeply relaxed than you are at the moment... And when I get to one...you will be able to step into that beautiful special place... You're going to be able to experience everything it has to offer...but most of all you will be so deeply relaxed... Ten...deeper and deeper now...nine...drifting and floating...deeper and deeper and deeper relaxed...eight...you begin to notice how very comfortable your body is beginning to feel and just how deeply relaxed you are...seven...six...deeper and deeper...five...four...three...two...one... You are now in your special place...just relax and enjoy... Take a few moments just to explore this beautiful place."*

So this is the part where you can insert your suggestion script. Remember that you can use one of the specific scripts that I have given you in this book, or have a go at making your own or changing mine.

"In a moment...I'm going to count from one to ten... And when I do...with each ascending number that you hear...you are going to feel more refreshed...more rejuvenated...and...as you feel more refreshed and more rejuvenated...all of the negative suggestions that you have been given...about feeling...heavy...tired...lethargic...will fade and be removed... And all of the positive suggestions will just be magnified... When I get to ten you will open your eyes and feel as though you have had a long...beautiful rest...full of energy...one...coming up now...two...feeling

more and more alert...three...four...five...more and more awake...six...seven...eight...nine....open your eyes and ten....feel great!"

If the problem that you are trying to resolve is still causing you issues after you have attempted to help yourself with these scripts, you should consider seeing a professional hypnotherapist. You can find more details on the MacKenzie Therapy & Training UK Website at www.richardmackenzie.co.uk.

History

"The years teach much which the days never knew."

Ralph Waldo Emerson (1803 – 1882)

History

There was much debate and deliberation as to whether I was going to include this chapter in the book. However I decided to, as I believe that the history of this marvellous art is just as fascinating a subject as trance itself. So get a cupper, sit back and enjoy this wonderful story of how it all came about!

Ancient history

Below is a brief description of the application of hypnosis and its origins with many cultures and races all over the ancient world.

Where did it all begin?

Hypnosis was used way before history records can show. People in places such as Africa, India, Australia and Egypt used rhythmic chanting, strained fixation and monotonous drums in order to enter a trance state; this happened regularly during their religious or healing ceremonies. Even though hypnotic trance was used it was not given its current name until 1842, when a Scottish surgeon called James Braid (1775-1860) took the Greek word "hypno" with means "to sleep" and coined the term hypnosis (see the section on Braid).

Recent history

Following is a detailed description of the application of and advances in hypnosis over the last three hundred years, from Dr Franz Anton Mesmer right up to the present day.

Franz Anton Mesmer

Hypnosis and hypnotherapy as we know it today, all started way back on the 23rd of May 1734, in Europe, at a place called Bodensee (Lake Constance) on the German-Swiss border, with the birth of Franz Anton Mesmer (1734-1815), the "Father of Hypnosis" (as he is known throughout the world of hypnosis and psychology).

He was raised in a Swiss-German family, in a small Swabian town called Iznang, and was the third of a family of nine children to be born to Anton Mesmer Senior and his wife. Unfortunately there is not a great deal known about the parents of Mesmer, except that his father was a gamekeeper and a forest warden for the Bishop of Constance. Both parents were very strong Catholics, and tried encouraging the young Mesmer into the priesthood, but to no avail.

Due to his father's work his parents were able to afford a decent and modest lifestyle for the family while living in Iznang. Mesmer at the age of 25 years went off to study law, but after one year he became bored of this subject and changed his educational direction to study for his medical doctorate at the University of Vienna. He received his medical degree in 1766 at the age of 32 years. His dissertation was on the influence of heavenly bodies on people's health, which he supposed to be by means of "animal gravity".

After qualifying Mesmer met a well-off aristocratic widow, who was ten years his senior, and soon after made her his wife. It was Frau Mesmer's connections that helped to build a prosperous practice for the recently qualified Mesmer.

In fact a young female relative of Frau Mesmer called Franziska Oesterlin, who suffered with a convulsive malady (nervous disorder), in 1773 became one of Mesmer's first ever clients and in treating her, Mesmer formed his profound belief that there was a "Quasi Magnetic Fluid" or "Cosmic Fluid" that was in the very air we inhale. And somehow this fluid after being inhaled absorbs itself into and through the nervous system and travels around the body via the blood. He believed that blockages of "Quasi Magnetic Fluid" in the nervous system could cause disease, illness and psychological problems.

He thought that this was the case with Frau Oesterlin, so he came up with a solution for apparently clearing these blockages and correcting the flow of "Quasi Magnetic Fluids" around the nervous system, and thus curing the disease. He had some strong magnets made for him by

Maximilien Hell, a professor of astronomy. He would pass these magnets over the blockages, thus correcting the ebb and flow of these "Cosmic Fluids". Mesmer and Hell soon got into a quarrel over who discovered the magnets and their phenomenon.

Mesmer then started using his hands as a substitute to start clearing these magnetic blockages and found it had the same effect, so the term "Animal Magnetism" was born and also the procedure known as Mesmerism.

He published his first book on the subject in 1775, called *Schreiben Uber die Magnetiker* (Memoirs about the Magnet). In February 1778 he moved with his wife to Paris, and founded a clinic with D'Eslon on the Place Vendome.

These unorthodox beliefs and methods of treating illness and disease used by Mesmer were frowned upon by most of his contemporaries, and within medical circles Mesmer was treated as an eccentric outsider, receiving a lot of flak for his beliefs. Nevertheless, clients and patients would still come from far and wide to see this wonderfully flamboyant individual, to experience this phenomenon, and to get treatment or a cure for their ailments.

In 1779 Mesmer published another book, *Memoire Sur La Decouverte Du Magnetisme Animal* (Memoirs about the Discovery of Animal Magnetism), which contained his ideas, but unfortunately this built him a reputation of an occultist and in 1784 after an investigation by the French government he was pronounced a fraud.

On 15th March 1815, at the age of 81 years, Franz Anton Mesmer died in Switzerland. Mesmer had apparently been told by a gypsy in Paris years earlier that this was the age at which he was going to die, and it has been said that he believed her and was prepared for the end to come.

The Marquis de Puysegur

The next chapter in the history of hypnosis is the story of one of Mesmer's very own students, whose name was the Marquis de Puysegur (1751-1825).

In 1784, at the age of 33 years, the Marquis de Puysegur discovered how to lead a client in to a deep trance state called "somnambulism", using relaxation and calming techniques. The term "somnambulism" is still widely used among hypnotherapists today in reference to a deep hypnotic trance state.

The Marquis de Puysegur was able to describe three cardinal features of this deep trance state or somnambulism; these were:

- Concentration of the senses on the operator,
- Acceptance of suggestion from the therapist,
- Amnesia for events in a trance.

Over two hundred years later these three theories of Puysegur still stand.

James Braid

In 1775 at Rylaw House in Fifeshire, James Braid, a future Scottish doctor and pioneer in hypnosis, was born.

It was in 1842 that Braid renamed magnetism and mesmerism to hypnosis and deemed it a psychological phenomenon. He got the word "hypno" from the Greek language; its meaning is "to sleep".

During his research into hypnosis he formed the following ideas, most of which still stand today:

- That hypnosis is a powerful tool which should be limited entirely to the medical and dental professions.
- That although hypnotism was capable of curing many diseases for which there had formally been no remedy, it nevertheless was no panacea and was only a medical tool which should be used in combination with other medical information, drugs, remedies, etc., in order to properly treat the patient.
- That in skilled hands there is no great danger associated with hypnotic treatment and neither is there pain or discomfort.

- That a good deal more study and research would be necessary to thoroughly understand a number of theoretical concepts regarding hypnosis.

James Braid died suddenly of a heart attack on March 25th 1860, at the age of 85 years. He maintained an interest in hypnotism throughout his life and made major contributions to the therapy that we use today.

James Esdaile

James Esdaile completed his first operation without using anaesthetic in Calcutta, India. The client was placed into a trance state in which he remained throughout the procedure. Esdaile assisted in 300 major operations and over a thousand minor ones. Esdaile's mortality rate was 5 percent. This was good at the time in India, as most other physicians had over a 50 percent death rate while completing the same operations as Esdaile was performing. This form of anaesthetic was soon put into second place due to the arrival of chloroform. It was thought easier to inject someone than to assist them to enter a trance state. Using hypnosis is still widely preferred as an alternative to conventional anaesthetics, especially in the dental profession.

Sigmund Freud

Sigmund Freud, born on 6th May 1856 in Freiberg, Moravia, got involved in hypnosis between 1883-1887 and practised for some time, but struggled with the technique and soon become bored. He abandoned hypnosis, saying that it was ineffective, and concentrated on developing psychoanalysis. Freud died on the 23rd September 1939 of cancer, from which he had been suffering since 1923, after making a big impact on the world of psychology.

The 20th century

During the last hundred years hypnosis has not stopped moving forward and has advanced to what you see today. During World War II it was widely used among psychiatrists and physicians to treat problems such as stress and battle fatigue. There have also been formed many councils, associations and organisations all over the world during the last century in order to assist the modern-day therapist to keep in touch with the latest information and discoveries. And most have a "Code of Ethics" for their members to follow.

The Hypnotism Act of 1952 was introduced to protect the public against dangerous practices in hypnotic shows, and the performer is still required to get a license granted in a Magistrates Court prior to such a show.

In 1970 the British Police tried experimenting with hypnosis for interviewing witnesses to certain crimes. Hypnosis was reported to be particularly effective in helping witnesses and victims recall detailed descriptions of criminals and perpetrators, relate the details of violent attacks and recall the scenarios immediately preceding certain accidents.

Milton H. Erickson

To give full credit to Milton H. Erickson's (1901-1980) life story in hypnosis, it deserves a complete section of its own, however here I will just explain briefly the outstanding achievements he made during his life. Prior to his death in 1980 Erickson certainly played his part in shaping hypnotherapy into what it is today.

Erickson was a psychotherapist who used hypnosis throughout his career to aid his clients' progression and recovery. He was excellent at intently observing people and rapidly building rapport with them. Metaphors, confusing statements, surprise, imagery, and humour were part of his vast range of therapeutic tools.

His methods of trance induction are nowadays referred to as Ericksonian hypnosis, and without a shadow of a doubt, he added another era to the history of modern hypnotherapy.

Hypnosis today

And so we arrive at the current day in the history of hypnosis. There are many leading figures and pioneers in the world of hypnotism today. And the story of hypnotism does not end here, quite the opposite in fact. There are new and exciting discoveries being made all the time and also "add-on" therapies that complement hypnotherapy, many of which have their roots in hypnosis. These are continually being developed, and the list is endless of the psychological problems, phobias and fears that can be put in their place by these well-founded therapies. Below are some examples:

- Stopping smoking
- Weight loss
- Improving low self-esteem and motivation
- Dealing with anxiety and panic
- Increasing athletic performance
- Curing procrastination (putting off doing something,, especially out of habitual carelessness or laziness)
- And curing phobias such as
    Fear of heights
    Fear of spiders, snakes and other animals
    Fear of public speaking
    Fear of enclosed spaces

As I said before, the list is endless, but this is enough to give you an idea of the vast possibilities of the therapeutic uses of hypnosis today.

Conclusion

In conclusion, the story of hypnosis starts way back before history was recorded. Down the line it has received contributions from many colourful characters and cultures, but the true fact is that hypnosis is really a fully natural phenomenon. It occurs to people all the time in everyday life and it has been harnessed in many ways over the years, by many individuals who wish to progress the phenomenon and bring it up to date in their time.

This is not by any means a full account of the history of hypnosis, more of a brief overview. There are many more characters who had their part to play, and should not be left out of this account. So below is a selection of a few:

John Elliotson (1791-1868)
Dr. Ambroise-Auguste Liebeault
Jean Martin Charcot (1825-1893)
Josef Breuer (1842-1925)
Dr. Eugene Azam
Milne Bramwell

Further Information

Richard MacKenzie and MacKenzie Therapy & Training UK
www.richardmackenzie.co.uk
+44 (0)845 2265 503

The General Hypnotherapy Register and The General
Hypnotherapy Standards Council (UK)
www.general-hypnotherapy-register.com
+44 (0)845 602 6031

The National Guild of Hypnotists (USA)
www.ngh.net
(603) 429 9438

The Freie Gesellschaft für Hypnose e.V. (Germany &
Europe)
www.hypnosegesellschaft.de
+49 (0)8734 93 24 00

Olf Stoiber Hypnotherapy and Hypnotherapist Training in
Europe
www.hypnoseberatung.de
+49 (0)8943 18 28 12

MacKenzie Therapy & Training UK does not represent or
endorse the accuracy or reliability of any of the information
provided by the above organisations.

ISBN 1-41204532-0